Puberty's Wild Ride

The Ups and Downs, Ins and Outs, Zigs and Zags of Growing Up

A publication of the Family Planning Council
Philadelphia, Pennsylvania

about this book

Published by the Family Planning Council
Philadelphia, Pennsylvania

Creative services provided by
Hollister Creative
Wynnewood, Pennsylvania
Marta McCave, writer
Joe Rademan, illustrator
Kim Landry and Martha Michaela Brown, editors
Heidi Karl, art director

To order copies of the book, contact:
Family Planning Council
215-985-2600
www.familyplanning.org

Library of Congress catalog card number: 978-0-9727746-1-1

introduction

This book is dedicated to you. Make it yours. Write in it, doodle on it, do the think-and-respond activities, mark the parts that have special meaning.

Share it too. Talk about it with family members and friends. Lend it to someone who needs it — but be sure to get it back! It can be your guidebook as you explore new territory on your journey from childhood to adulthood.

Exploring this new territory can be exciting, but it can be a little scary too. No one who enters puberty has ever been there before. It looks and feels very different. And as you travel through, you realize that the world isn't changing — you are! Your body is morphing from child to adult. You are forming new kinds of relationships. And you are starting to separate from your parents.*

Change is exciting, but it can be scary, too.

This book is meant to take some of the scariness out of growing up. We'll talk about what's going on with your mind, body and emotions. We'll explain how these changes affect the way you relate to your family and to boys and girls your own age.

While we are giving you a lot of information, we can't possibly tell you everything you want to know in these 100+ pages. So we've added a list of other helpful books and websites at the end.

It's important to have information that you can trust when you have so many big decisions ahead of you. But information is not enough. You also need a real live person who will listen when you feel confused, squeeze you when you need a hug, and cheer you on when you're doing well. For that kind of personal support, we urge you to turn to a trusted adult — your parent or the parent of a friend, an older sister, brother or other relative, a clergy member or a neighbor you know well. Of course, friends your age can provide support. But at times it truly helps to talk with someone older who has "been there" — and survived!

*Note: Wherever you see the word "parents" we are talking about the adult person or persons who take care of you. We realize that children are raised in many kinds of families.

chapter 1: me + my changing body

chapter 2: me + my growing mind

chapter 3: me + my friends

chapter 4: me + my sexuality

table of contents

chapter 5: me + my safety

chapter 6: me + my family

chapter 7: me + my school

chapter 8: me + my world

chapter 1

me + my changing body

puberty

what happens to boys

what happens to girls

menstruation

"normal" development

body image

health care

nutrition

problems with food

obesity

fitness

personal grooming

skin care

puberty

Some people pronounce it "PEW-ber-tee." Others call it "POO-ber-tee." Whichever way they say it, they're talking about changes that happen to every boy and girl, usually between the ages of 10 and 15. As your body changes, and you become a young man or woman, you are able to make a baby.

Puberty doesn't happen all of a sudden — it's a gradual process that takes three or four years. Girls usually start and finish puberty ahead of the boys their age.

The changes begin with a pea-sized part of your brain called the pituitary (pit-TEW-it-ary) gland. One day — no one knows exactly why — this gland begins sending chemicals called hormones (HOR-moanz) into your bloodstream. Hormones are messengers. They tell other parts of the body to develop or behave in a certain way.

Puberty makes it possible for you to create a baby.

Pituitary hormones tell girls' bodies to begin releasing eggs from the ovaries and boys' bodies to begin making sperm. Together, one egg and one sperm can create a baby.

These changes are going on inside your body, so you can't see them. But other hormones are changing you in ways you *can* see.

During puberty, girls develop breasts and grow hair in their armpits and around the genital (JEN-it-al) area between their legs. Boys' sex organs grow larger and they, too, grow hair — on their faces as well as their bodies. Boys' voices also change, becoming deeper.

Both boys and girls rapidly grow taller during puberty. Boys might grow as much as eight inches. Girls generally don't get as tall, but most start their growth spurt before the boys do.

Body shapes also change. During childhood, girls and boys are about equal in muscle size and strength. During puberty, boys add more muscle than most girls, especially in their arms, chest and shoulders. Girls begin to develop a feminine body shape, with wider hips and a smaller waist than boys.

sex organs of boys

The **penis** (PEE-nis) is the organ used in urinating and in sexual activity. You may hear slang* words for penis such as dick, cock, pecker and prick. The rounded tip of the penis is called the glans. The long part is called the shaft.

All boys are born with a loose foreskin covering the end of the penis. As babies, many boys have their foreskin removed by a health care provider or specially trained religious person in a procedure called a **circumcision** (SIR-cum-SIH-shun).

The soft sac of wrinkly skin behind the penis is called the **scrotum** (SCRO-tum). It contains and protects the testicles.

Boys have two **testicles** (TESS-tickles), which are walnut-sized glands that produce sperm. Slang for testicles includes nuts, balls and jewels.

Sperm cells travel from the testicle to the **vas deferens** (vas-DEF-a-renz), where they are stored. The seminal vesicles and the prostate gland produce the fluid that combines with sperm to make **semen** (SEE-men). This is the milky mixture that gets ejaculated during sexual activity. A slang term for semen is cum.

Ejaculation occurs through a tube inside the penis called the **urethra** (your-EE-thra), the same tube through which urine passes out of the body.

We've given slang terms as well as proper terms for some organs, but you should know that many people find the slang words offensive.

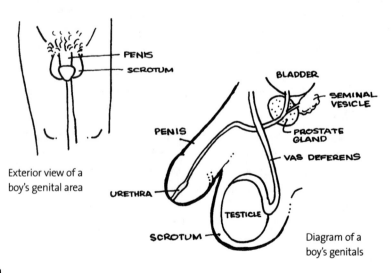

Exterior view of a
boy's genital area

Diagram of a
boy's genitals

what happens to boys

For most boys, the first sign of puberty is that their sex organs — the penis, scrotum and testicles — grow larger. A grown man's penis is usually between 3 ¼ inches and 4 ¼ inches in length. (It gets temporarily longer and thicker during an erection.)

You may worry about whether your penis is big enough. Boys hear many jokes that suggest a large penis is a sign of manliness. Laugh at that suggestion. Penis size has nothing to do with how you feel or function as a man.

During puberty — usually between ages 10 and 15 — your entire body will grow tremendously. In addition to getting taller, the average boy gains 40 pounds. Your voice will change as your voice box, or larynx (LAHR-inks) gets bigger. Your voice may crack or squeak for awhile, but will soon deepen.

You'll also be growing hair on many parts of your body. Before the pubic (PEW-bik) hair starts to grow on and around your sex organs, you may see raised bumps on the skin surface where little hairs will poke through. You may also notice little bumps on the skin of the penis and scrotum. These are oil and sweat glands, and they, too, are normal. Your skin and hair become more oily during puberty, and your body sweats more. (For advice on personal grooming during puberty, see page 23.)

The first sign of puberty in boys: their sex organs get larger.

Increased male sex hormones will make you feel stronger romantic and sexual longings, which can seem bewildering and even scary. Hormones also cause more frequent erections (e-RECK-shuns) in nearly all boys during puberty. An erection (slang: boner, hard-on) occurs when blood rushes into the veins and spongy tissue in the penis, causing the shaft to get temporarily longer, thicker and harder. It's also common for a boy to have nocturnal emissions, also called wet dreams, during which semen is released as he sleeps.

Don't freak out if you discover a small lump developing beneath one or both of your nipples. You're not turning into a girl! Male breast development occurs in about 40 percent of boys. It usually disappears in about a year.

While all of these changes are normal, you may have questions or concerns. It often helps to talk with an older boy or a trusted adult who has "been there."

3

sex organs of girls

The **clitoris** (CLIT-or-iss) is a small pea-shaped bump that is the center of sexual sensation for females. It is part of the **vulva** area between a girl's legs. The clitoris is hidden by protective folds or flaps of soft skin called the outer and inner lips or **labia** (LAY-bee-ya). The labia also protects the opening to the urethra, through which urine passes out of the body, and the vaginal opening.

The **vagina** (vuh-JY-na) is the passageway from the uterus to the outside of the body. Menstrual blood and babies pass through the vaginal opening. You may hear slang* words for vagina such as cunt or pussy. You may also have heard about a thin skin membrane called the **hymen** (HY-men) that is just inside the vaginal opening and partly blocks it. A common slang word for hymen is cherry. People used to say the presence of a

hymen meant that the girl hadn't yet had sexual intercourse. But some girls are born without a hymen and in others it gets stretched through strenuous activity before they become sexually active.

Deep inside a girl's body is her **uterus** (YOU-ter-us) or **womb** (WOOM), the place where menstrual blood comes from, and where a developing baby grows until it is ready to be born. The uterus is shaped and sized like an upside-down pear. It is connected to the vagina by the **cervix** (SIR-vicks), a small opening that can stretch very wide to let a baby through at birth.

Ovaries (OH-vahr-eez) are the two strawberry-sized organs that produce and store egg cells. Eggs travel from the ovaries to the uterus through **fallopian** (Full-OH-pee-yan) tubes.

Keep in mind that many people find the slang words for sex organs offensive.

Exterior view of a
girl's genital area

Diagram of a
girl's genitals

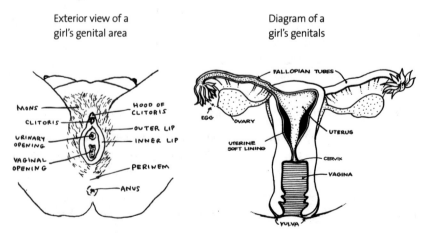

A girl's sex organs take up very little room inside her body. Cut a four-inch circle out of paper. Hold it about an inch below your belly button. That's all the space they need!

4

what happens to girls

If you're a girl, "breast buds" are apt to be the first sign that puberty has begun. Your breasts will seem to sprout from your chest, becoming small mounds. You'll buy your first bra.

Next, you will start to find hair in your armpits and curly pubic (PEW-bik) hair in your genital (JEN-it-al) area. Later you will start to menstruate (MEN-strew-ate). Some girls have their first monthly menstrual period at age 9; some don't have their first period until age 16. (More on menstruation: page 7.)

While you're quickly gaining height over the puberty years, you'll also be gaining weight. Don't be alarmed! It's normal and healthy. The average girl gains 25 pounds. You'll notice that your weight isn't as evenly spread around as it was in childhood. More will attach to your breasts and hips.

The first sign of puberty in girls: they begin to develop breasts.

You may worry about whether your breasts are big enough or too big. Girls hear a lot of rude and stupid talk about breast size. The truth is, breast size says no more about who you are than the size of your big toe. Your breast size, whatever it turns out to be, will not affect how you feel or function as a woman.

You'll probably find it exciting to be going through these changes, but you may not be too thrilled about some other side-effects of puberty: Your skin and hair will become much more oily, and your body will sweat more. (For advice on personal grooming during puberty, see page 23.) You may have occasional discharge from your vagina (this is a natural cleansing process, but ask your health care provider if anything about the discharge concerns you). Increased female sex hormones will make you feel stronger romantic and sexual feelings, which can seem bewildering and even scary.

Your changing body may attract more attention than you would like from men and boys. Whether it's compliments or rude sexual comments, chances are the sudden attention will make you at least a little uncomfortable. Other girls or a trusted adult may be able to offer advice about coping. You have a right to grow into womanhood without being teased or harassed about your body. (See hallway harassment: page 127.)

5

menstruation facts and feelings

Menstruation facts:

- All together, a few tablespoons (1 to 3 ounces) of bloody discharge flows out of your vagina over the three to eight days of your period.

- A menstrual period comes every 21 to 40 days. Some girls' periods occur very regularly; say, every 28 days. Other girls find that the time between their periods varies a lot. It is common for pre-teens and teens to have irregular periods.

- You count your menstrual cycle from the first day of your period. That's Day 1. A 28-day cycle is one in which menstruation begins again on the 28th day.

- Some girls experience PMS – Premenstrual Syndrome – in the days leading up to their period. There can be physical symptoms such as increased acne or breast tenderness, as well as mental symptoms such as being moody or crying. PMS symptoms stop when your period starts. Tell your health care provider if you need relief.

Menstruation feelings:

When it comes to menstruation, "just the facts" is not enough. You're going to have feelings — maybe even strong feelings — about this change. One good way to sort out your feelings is to talk with a trusted older woman, such as your mother, an older sister or cousin, aunt, grandmother, teacher or counselor. You could ask:

- How old were you when you had your first period?

- Where were you when you first discovered the blood? What did you do then?

- How did you feel about getting your period? Do you still feel the same way?

- Do you get PMS? What are your symptoms? How do you handle them?

What else do you want to know? Write down a few more questions here:

_____

_____

_____

_____

menstruation

Menstruation (men-strew-AY-shun) is one sign that a girl is becoming a woman. In the U.S., the average age that a girl first gets her period is $12^1/2$ years. You may begin earlier or later.

Menstruation is part of a continuing process called the menstrual cycle. The cycle begins with ovulation (AHV-u-lay-shun), when one of the ovaries releases an egg. The egg travels down a fallopian tube to the uterus. (See diagram on page 4.)

When you get a menstrual period, it's because your uterus has built up a supply of blood and tissue that would be needed if your egg was fertilized by a sperm and you became pregnant. When pregnancy doesn't occur, your body gets rid of the unfertilized egg as well as the unneeded blood and tissue by releasing it from the uterus into the vagina and out of the body.

To absorb the discharge, most women choose pads or tampons. A pad, also called a sanitary napkin, is a strip of cotton, usually with a plastic lining, that's worn inside the underpants. A tampon is a peg-shaped plug of soft cotton that fits into the vagina and expands as it soaks up fluid. When it's inserted correctly (follow the directions inside the box or ask a trusted woman to instruct you), you won't feel the tampon at all.

Menstrual periods typically begin at around age 12 ¹/₂.

Whether you choose pads or tampons, you'll need a fresh one several times a day, especially during the first couple days when flow is heaviest. The flow will stop in three to eight days.

You may get cramps in your lower belly or back when you are menstruating, or you may feel just fine. Cramps can range from mild discomfort to pain. If you need a pain reliever, ask your health care provider to recommend one. It is rare for a girl to feel so uncomfortable that she cannot keep up with her regular activities, including sports.

One final word about tampons: A rare but serious disease called Toxic Shock Syndrome has been linked to tampon use. To reduce your risk, change your tampon regularly during the day and use a pad instead overnight. Call your health care provider immediately if you develop any of these symptoms while using tampons: fever, nausea and vomiting, diarrhea, dizziness, or a painless, red sunburn-like rash.

"normal" development

Chances are the person sitting next to you in class is either more developed than you are, or less developed than you are. It's actually quite normal to wonder, "Are we both 'normal'?"

The answer is almost always "yes." Each person starts puberty at a different time and changes at a different speed. And whether you go through puberty early or late has nothing to do with how your adult body will look and perform when it's fully formed.

If puberty hasn't begun for you, and you're worried about it, talk with your health care provider. A trained person can find out whether you are maturing normally. He or she will look at the development of your sex organs, and may also take X-rays of your wrists and other bones. It may then be possible to predict roughly when you will enter puberty.

You could also ask your parents when they started puberty. You are likely to start at about the same age.

Here are some other "normal" occurrences in puberty:

Each boy and girl moves through puberty at a different speed.

• Just before entering puberty, you may find that your body has some added fat. The fat usually goes away during puberty when you are growing quickly.

• The shape of your face will change during puberty as your lower jaw becomes longer. You'll look more like an adult and less like a child.

• In girls, one breast or nipple may be larger than the other. In boys, one testicle (usually the left) may hang lower than the other.

• Puberty hormones can leave some boys feeling sore and tender in the area around their nipples. In most cases, it's just temporary.

9

uniquely y⊙u

Don't like the way you look? Well, there must be something to like in the many features that make up your appearance. Using the list below, mark "like" or "don't" beside each feature. If you mark "like," write what you like about this feature on the line provided.

If you mark "don't," write what you can do to change or play down this feature. If there's nothing you can do about it, write instead the name of a person you admire who has the same "problem" feature.

Feature	Like	Don't	Comment
Eyes	☐	☐	_____
Nose	☐	☐	_____
Mouth	☐	☐	_____
Teeth	☐	☐	_____
Chin	☐	☐	_____
Cheeks	☐	☐	_____
Ears	☐	☐	_____
Skin	☐	☐	_____
Hair	☐	☐	_____
Chest	☐	☐	_____
Waist	☐	☐	_____
Hips	☐	☐	_____
Arms	☐	☐	_____
Hands	☐	☐	_____
Thighs	☐	☐	_____
Knees	☐	☐	_____
Calves	☐	☐	_____
Feet	☐	☐	_____

body image

Many teenagers are unhappy with the size and shape of their bodies. They think they're too fat. Or too skinny. Or too short. Or too tall. They find fault with their noses, their teeth, their eyes, their hair.

It's normal to want to look attractive. But our society's emphasis on looks can be harmful. Sadly, many women think they have to have a fashion model's face and shape in order to feel good and be loved. Many men who are not naturally strong and athletic sadly think they are "less manly" than others.

The way you look is unique — so enjoy being special.

Every year Americans spend millions of dollars to improve their looks. Commercials on TV always try to make us think we should be doing more to beautify our hair, skin and body. Think about it, though: It's all just aimed at getting us to buy more stuff.

In truth, healthy, attractive, happy people come in all sizes and shapes. Unless you are an identical twin, your appearance is unique — yours alone to feel good about for its one-of-a-kind specialness. Keep these thoughts in mind when you stand in front of a mirror.

Your looks are a combination of traits you inherited from your parents. But you're not a finished work—yet. As you go through the rapid and sometimes uneven growth phases of puberty, try to think of your appearance as a work in progress. Like the Ugly Duckling in the children's story, you just might turn out to be a swan.

Meanwhile, you have to deal with the fact that teens can and do say some really mean things about each other's appearance. And sometimes the cruelest people are the ones with the biggest inner doubts about their own looks. If you're on the receiving end of that cruelty, try not to take it to heart. Even if you don't turn out to be a swan, you'll find as you get older that ordinary-looking people with good hearts are more admired than beautiful faces.

you've got questions

Boys and girls going through puberty have a lot of questions about their changing bodies. If you are too embarrassed to ask the questions, you may be causing yourself needless worry. Before your next checkup, use this page to write down five things you want to know about your body. Try to find the answers in this book. If you can't get the answers you need here, take this page with you the next time you have a checkup. Hand it to your health care provider.

Five things I'd like to know about my body:

1. _____

_____

2. _____

_____

3. _____

_____

4. _____

_____

5. _____

_____

health care

With all the changes your body is going through during puberty, it's especially important to *get a checkup at least once a year*. In addition to the general body check you've been getting since childhood, the health care provider will now be examining your developing sex organs.

Boys: The health care provider will feel your testicles, scrotum and penis to check for lumps and/or pain that could indicate a problem. *Ask the health care provider to show you how to check your own testicles for lumps.* Sometimes the health care provider will also feel inside your anus to check for rectal lumps.

Girls: The health care provider will feel your breasts and your pelvic area, checking for lumps, swelling, and/or pain that could indicate a problem. Some doctors also may do an "internal" pelvic exam, feeling inside your vagina to check the internal sex organs. A vaccine to prevent most types of cervical cancer and genital warts is now available, and your health care provider may talk to you about it. To be most effective, the vaccine needs to be given to young adolescents, ages 9 and up, before they have their first sexual relationship.

What to expect when you go for a checkup.

Whether you're a boy or a girl, the health care professional may ask you some very personal questions. For example, you may be asked if you've had sexual intercourse. Always tell the truth. (Anyone who is sexually active should be tested for certain diseases: see page 79.) Feel free to ask the health care provider any questions you may have.

Note: If you are taking a prescription drug—for allergies, acne, anything!— be sure to tell any health care professional you go to for any reason. They need to know because otherwise they might prescribe a drug for you that could cause a bad reaction with a drug you're already taking. Also, never share your prescriptions with friends or take a drug prescribed for someone else. A drug that helps one person could seriously harm another. Only a trained medical professional can make the right prescription choice for you.

food mix & match

A healthy diet is an exciting diet with lots of variety every day. You can mix in many, many different types of foods as long as you match the foods to all five of the major food groups:

Grains   **Vegetables**   **Fruits**   **Milk & Dairy**   **Meat & Beans**

For each "grocery bag" on this page, write next to each food item which group it belongs to. *Hint:* Each bag contains one example from each of the five food groups.

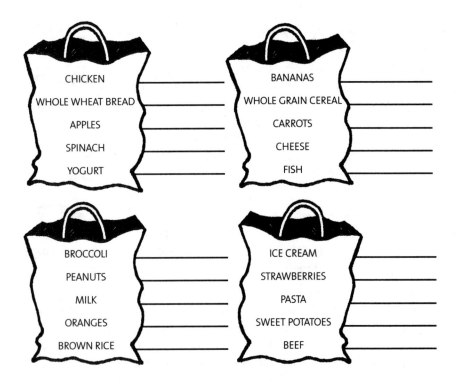

CHICKEN _____
WHOLE WHEAT BREAD _____
APPLES _____
SPINACH _____
YOGURT _____

BANANAS _____
WHOLE GRAIN CEREAL _____
CARROTS _____
CHEESE _____
FISH _____

BROCCOLI _____
PEANUTS _____
MILK _____
ORANGES _____
BROWN RICE _____

ICE CREAM _____
STRAWBERRIES _____
PASTA _____
SWEET POTATOES _____
BEEF _____

Note: Girls need to make sure they get plenty of calcium and Vitamin D to build strong bones. Check out www.bestbonesforever.gov to learn more.

During puberty, your body is growing so rapidly that good nutrition is more important than ever. Poor nutrition can interfere with growth. And too much high-calorie food can lead to obesity and health problems. Here's a simple guide to healthy eating:

• Eat a variety of nutritious foods (5 to 9 servings a day of fruits and veggies, plus whole-grain cereals and breads, fish, poultry, low-fat milk). They contain the fuels your body needs: vitamins, minerals, protein, fiber.

• Avoid junk food (the salty, sugary, greasy stuff). Junk adds fat to your body without giving it enough of the fuel it needs to grow and perform well. At fast-food restaurants, make simple substitutions such as grilled meat instead of fried, salad instead of french fries, water instead of soda.

• Eat only when you are hungry; stop eating when you've had enough, even if there is still food on your plate.

It sounds simple, and it *would* be – *if* the only signals to eat came from inside our bodies. But in fact we get many of our signals to eat from the outside world: from ads on TV, candy displays, fast-food restaurants on every corner. These signals tell us to eat too much, too often, and to choose foods that are high in sugar and fat. Many people respond to the signals. That's one reason so many Americans are overweight and prone to health problems like heart disease, diabetes and cancer.

Eat well, you fuel your body. Eat junk, you trash your body.

If you are overweight, you may be tempted to "go on a diet." For most young people, this is a bad idea. It can set up a lifelong pattern of overeating followed by dieting. Instead, learn now how to eat well. Start by cutting out the junk food and drinking water instead of soda. Reduce the portion size of nutritious foods that are high in calories, such as red meats and cheese. Snack on fresh fruits and veggies. Don't be fooled into buying the "diet pills" you see advertised because they don't work. Prescription diet pills you get from a health care provider work for some people but they have nasty side-effects and are dangerous if taken by the wrong person or in the wrong amount.

If you want to gain weight or "bulk up," increase the amount you eat at meals, eat more frequently, or both. Snack on nutrition-packed, high-calorie foods like dried fruits and nuts. Talk to your health care provider before trying any supplements or pills that claim to put on pounds. Some are dangerous.

15

the food-feelings connection

You eat when you're hungry, but do you also eat when you're happy or sad or bored or angry? Keep a log of your feelings before and after eating between-meal snacks for two days.

Based on what you learn reading page 17, do you think you could be developing a problem with food? If so, what could you do now to head it off?

Day One

My snack was: _____

Feelings before: _____

Feelings after: _____

My snack was: _____

Feelings before: _____

Feelings after: _____

Day Two

My snack was: _____

Feelings before: _____

Feelings after: _____

My snack was: _____

Feelings before: _____

Feelings after: _____

problems with food

A serious problem with food is called an eating disorder. These disorders often begin to develop during puberty. A person's feelings about food somehow get out of whack, and they abuse food. The people most likely to suffer from eating disorders are teenage girls, but some boys have food problems too.

Food becomes the most important thing in life for people who have an eating disorder. They think about eating, or about not eating, all the time. They use food to reward and to punish themselves.

One serious eating disorder is anorexia (an-or-EX-ee-ah). People who have this disorder starve themselves to be thin. Yet every time they look in the mirror, they see a fat person. Anorexics eventually become very sick; some starve themselves to death.

Food can become the most important thing in life.

People who have the eating disorder called bulimia (bull-EEM-ee-ah) will "binge"—eat a huge amount of food in one sitting—then "purge" by forcing themselves to throw up or take a lot of laxatives (drugs that cause bowel movements). Bulimia can make a person very sick.

Obesity (oh-BEE-sih-tee), becoming dangerously overweight, can result from another disorder, compulsive overeating. Compulsive eaters feel addicted to food the way an alcoholic is addicted to liquor. They may try diet after diet but never keep the weight off. Obesity strains the heart and causes many other health problems.

Some experts say that more than half the teens who have an eating disorder also have at least one parent with a food problem. That can make it difficult to find help. If you need help with an eating disorder, talk with a trusted adult, call the National Eating Disorder Association helpline at 1-800-931-2237 or visit Overeaters Anonymous online at www.oa.org to find a support meeting near you. You also may find help at a community hospital.

slimming tips

You lose weight when you burn more calories than you eat. To find out how many calories you should be eating each day, ask your health care provider or visit the Web site www.MyPyramid.gov and fill in the form.

Here are some ways to cut down on calories and get more exercise. Maybe you can't do all of these things right away. But you can make a start. Put a check mark next to three things you could do starting today:

Eating at home

☐ Read the nutrition labels on the foods you eat to find out what the serving size is and how many calories each serving contains.

☐ Never eat while watching TV or surfing the Internet. You aren't paying attention to the food and will eat too much.

☐ Eat slowly at meals and stop eating once you're full. Leftovers can be eaten later when you are hungry again.

☐ Drink water or nonfat milk instead of sodas and juices, which are very high in sugar and contain a lot of calories.

☐ Eat breakfast because it helps you burn food properly all day.

☐ If you crave a salty snack, choose a small bag of popcorn or pretzels instead of potato chips.

Eating at restaurants

☐ The portion sizes at most restaurants are much larger than anyone should eat. So plan to take half your meal home to eat later. Or, go with a friend and split the meal. You'll save calories and dollars!

☐ Avoid fried foods and instead choose broiled, grilled or baked options.

☐ Ask for sauces, salad dressings and croutons to be served on the side so you can add only a small amount.

☐ Try a bite before you add any high-calorie condiment like butter, sour cream, mayonnaise or ketchup. The food might taste better without it!

☐ If you can substitute fruit or salad for French fries, do it. If you can't resist the fries, order the smallest size.

Exercising

☐ Plan on at least one hour a day for active fun. Kids can burn 1,000 calories a day just by playing outside!

☐ With friends you could toss a Frisbee, jump rope, go for a walk or jog, or put on some music and teach each other your best dance moves.

☐ Join an intramural sports teams at school or sign up for one of the activities your local recreation center is offering.

obesity

Nearly 19 of every 100 young people ages 6 to 10 are severely overweight or "obese." That's triple the rate of 30 years ago, according to the federal government. Obesity is dangerous because having too much fat on your body makes you more likely to suffer from serious health problems, such as high blood pressure, high cholesterol, type 2 diabetes, liver disease and sleep disorders. Obesity can also lead to some mental health problems like depression.

If you are overweight, now is the time to start changing the unhealthy eating habits and lack of exercise that caused you to get too fat. It will be easier to slim down now, when you are young and still growing, than it will be later in life. And good habits started now will make it easier to stay healthy, because most adults follow the same eating and exercise habits they developed as teens.

Eating right may be hard at first. But being fat is hard, too.

The best way to start fighting obesity is to act like the boss and owner of your body. Learn what your body needs to be healthy. Then decide what you're going to feed it and how you're going to exercise it.

Eating right isn't always easy because we are tempted to eat the sugary, salty, greasy fast foods and junk foods that seem to be all around us. And exercising isn't as easy as sitting in front of a TV or video game player.

But it's not easy to be fat either. Mean people tease you. The clothes you'd like to wear may not fit you. You get out of breath and sweaty doing everyday things like climbing stairs — things that are easy for slimmer people.

The way you have been eating is a habit. So is the way you have been spending your free time. Changing any habit is hard at first, but it gets easier as you stick with it over days and weeks and months. After only a few months the new healthy way you eat will become a habit. If you spend fewer hours sitting and more hours moving your body, that will become a habit too.

It can be easier to change your habits when you have the support of family and friends. So ask them to support your efforts and encourage you. One or more of them may want to join you. If so, you may enjoy having a healthy habits buddy with whom to share your struggles and success.

impr⊚ving fitness

Here's one way to tell if your physical fitness needs improvement: Time your resting heart rate. A physically fit person typically has a resting heart rate of 40 to 60 beats per minute. The range for non-athletes over 10 years old is 60 to 100 beats per minute.*

To determine your resting heart rate, check your pulse before you get out of bed in the morning. Watching a clock that has a second hand, feel and count the number of beats in 10 seconds. Multiply that count by 6. The product is pulses per minute — your resting heart rate. To get the most accurate rate,

repeat this count on three mornings and average the results.

To improve your fitness, you have to get moving. Turn off the TV set, get off the couch and do something active. It doesn't really matter what you do as long as it involves movement and you enjoy it. Doing something you enjoy is important because if you don't enjoy it you won't keep doing it.

Use the space below to explore your options for being active.

Active things I know I like:

☐ walk

☐ ride bicycle

☐ jog

☐ swim

☐ dance

☐ exercise class

☐ roller skate/blade

☐ skateboard

☐ ice skate

☐ sport _____

☐ sport _____

☐ sport _____

☐ sport _____

☐ sport _____

Active things I'd like to try:

walk ☐

ride bicycle ☐

jog ☐

swim ☐

dance ☐

exercise class ☐

roller skate/blade ☐

skateboard ☐

ice skate ☐

_____ sport ☐

_____ sport ☐

_____ sport ☐

_____ sport ☐

_____ sport ☐

* Source: www.nlm.nih.gov/medlineplus, a service of the U.S. National Library of Medicine and the National Institutes of Health

fitness

When it comes to fitness, you are very lucky. You're at the perfect age to make frequent exercise a habit that will lead to a lifetime of fitness and good health.

You feel better when you're fit. You have energy for school, playing and everything else you do. You sleep well and have a good appetite. You're also less likely to get sick.

Fitness is a combination of three things:

- **Endurance.** A person with good endurance can play longer without getting tired. You should be able to do your favorite aerobic (air-O-bik) exercise — running, dancing, biking, skating, swimming, whatever it is — for at least 20 minutes at a time without stopping. Aerobic (air-OH-bik) exercise makes your heart and lungs work harder, which strengthens them. Plan some form of aerobic exercise at least three times a week. If you can't last the full 20 minutes, just try to last 30 seconds longer tomorrow than you lasted today.

- **Flexible joints and muscles.** A person with a flexible body can reach, twist and bend without stiffness, pain or strain. Slow stretching exercises increase your flexibility. They're also important as a warmup before you do any fast exercise, to make a muscle injury less likely. You can stretch almost any time — even while you're watching TV!

For a lifetime of fitness, make exercise a habit now.

- **Strong muscles.** A person who has a strong body can do more and do it better. When you increase your strength you can run faster, jump higher and carry more weight. A strong body also uses food better, burning it for fuel instead of storing it as fat. To build strength, do exercises that use the body's own weight for resistance — bent-leg sit-ups and push-ups, for example. Using barbells and other weights can be harmful to young teens.

Some boys who want very badly to "bulk up" with extra muscle abuse drugs called steroids. These drugs can seriously—and permanently—damage the kidneys and the heart. That's why all amateur and professional sports organizations ban steroids and disqualify athletes found to be using them.

it "ads" up

Do you have dandruff? Bad breath? Body odor?

American teens are bombarded with messages — in magazine articles, on TV ads — telling them they better buy "Brand X," or else!

Or else: That flaky white stuff on your shoulders will make your date gasp in horror.

Or else: You better not exhale for fear that your first kiss will be postponed indefinitely.

Or else: The toxic fumes coming from your armpits will cause a mass evacuation.

Ads exaggerate, of course. But exaggerating can be fun. Try it. Write a "sell line" to go with each of the cartoons. Make up a name for the product you're pitching.

_____

_____

_____   _____

_____   _____

personal grooming

During puberty, your sweat glands become more active. You perspire more in places where you have many sweat glands: under your arms, the bottoms of your feet and between your legs. The changes that take place during puberty also make your sweat have a stronger smell than it had when you were a child. Uh, oh... B.O.

To control body odor, take a bath or shower every day. You also may want to use a deodorant to reduce body odor and/or an anti-perspirant to control wetness (sweating). Some products are a combination of deodorant and anti-perspirant (read the product label). Whichever products you use, remember they're no substitute for soap and water.

You may also find that your hair needs to be washed more often during puberty. Blame over-active oil glands again — the ones on your scalp.

Speaking of hair, girls may choose to remove underarm and leg hair by shaving or other hair-removal methods. Most boys don't need to shave facial hair until their mid- to late-teens.

You sweat more, and it smells worse, so take a shower.

Boys: Poor hygiene can lead to annoying fungal infections such as "jock itch," a rash in the genital area, and "athlete's foot," a fungus that thrives on hot, moist feet. To avoid fungal infections, keep your genital area and feet clean and dry. Avoid tight clothing and always make sure your socks, jock straps and underwear are clean. For uncircumcised boys, good grooming includes keeping the foreskin of the penis clean, washing away the whitish smegma (SMEG-ma) that accumulates there.

Girls: Don't use vaginal deodorant sprays. They can irritate the delicate skin. It's normal to have some discharge from the vagina at certain times of your menstrual cycle. Very strong odor coming from your vagina can be a sign of infection; you should see a health care professional. And when you use the toilet, be careful to wipe from the front to the rear. Germs from the anus can cause infections if they get into the vagina.

23

skin myths and facts

Myth or fact?

1. If you wash your face a lot you won't get blackheads.

2. Chocolate, cola drinks and fatty foods such as French fries cause acne.

3. Sun helps control acne by drying out oily skin.

1. Myth! The black part of the blackhead is sebum, not dirt. When it comes into contact with air, it turns black. Washing with an abrasive soap won't help, and it can hurt. African-American boys and girls need to be especially careful because abrasive scrubbing might permanently discolor their dark complexions.

2. Myth! There is no scientific evidence that junk foods cause acne or make it worse.

3. Myth! Sun actually increases the oil production, one more reason to limit your exposure to the sun's rays.

skin care

Pimples. Whiteheads. Blackheads. Suddenly they seem to be staring back at you from the mirror.

Eight out of every 10 people get pimples and acne during puberty. If one of your parents had acne as a teen, there's a good chance you will, too.

During puberty, the oil glands under your skin start making more sebum (SEE-bum), a white, oily liquid that rises to the skin surface through tiny ducts. Sebum's purpose is to keep your skin moist. But whiteheads or blackheads can result if the sebum gets stuck in the ducts.

If a duct gets infected, it becomes the red, swollen, pus-filled thing we call acne, a pimple, or a zit. In its most severe form, acne can involve big inflamed lumps called cysts.

Ducts often get infected when you squeeze a whitehead or blackhead to pop out the gunk—especially if your face and hands weren't cleaned before you started. Squeezing can make the duct break, releasing the infected sebum under your skin and spreading infection around your face.

Eight out of every 10 people get pimples during puberty.

The skin of some African-Americans is prone to abnormal scar tissue called keloids. In people who get keloids, popping a pimple can leave a bad scar.

If you have a mild case of acne, you may want to try a cream or lotion that contains benzoyl peroxide. Such products can be found in any drug store. If you have a more serious case, see your health care professional. New acne-fighting medicines are available with a health care provider's prescription.

To keep acne in check, wash your face daily with a mild soap and avoid cosmetics that have oil in them.

And remember that — annoying as acne can be — too much sun is far more dangerous to your skin's health than a few zits. Be sure to apply a sunscreen whenever you're going to be in the sun. And don't use tanning beds — using them can lead to skin cancer.

chapter 2

me + my growing mind

ups + downs
depression
stress
boys have feelings
girls have brains
optimism

are you moody?

Use this page to keep a log of your moods for one week. Each day, identify at least one mood you felt strongly. Think about and write down what caused that mood to start and stop.

Day One _____

_____

Day Two _____

_____

Day Three _____

_____

Day Four _____

_____

Day Five _____

_____

Day Six _____

_____

Day Seven _____

_____

What did you learn this week about your moods? When you get in a bad mood now can you think of things to do to change your mood?

ups + downs

Have you noticed yourself crying or laughing for no reason? Or suddenly yelling at someone without knowing why you're angry? And just as suddenly feeling giddy and silly?

Many boys and girls your age become very moody during puberty. If you feel like your emotions are riding a really wild roller coaster, it's because they are! So many changes are going on inside your body, your feelings can get tossed high and low, zig-zag, switchback and loop-the-loop.

The good news and the bad news is the same: Many of these mood swings are beyond your control. They are caused by the sex hormones traveling through your body. You can't be blamed for your moodiness, but you can't just decide to snap out of it either.

You may feel like you're on a really wild roller coaster.

During puberty, the changes you're going through can make you worried, anxious, hopeless or sad. Sometimes an important event like a birthday or a big party can send your emotions into orbit. Even if you've been looking forward to the occasion for a long time, you might be surprised to find yourself picking a fight with your parents or locking yourself in your room when the day finally arrives.

This book can't make your hormones stop messing with your emotions. But hopefully, as you read on you will find comfort in the fact that every boy or girl in your age group, everywhere in the world, is going through the same changes.

Some teens make the mistake of taking out their bad feelings on themselves. They may overeat or starve themselves, abuse drugs or drink alcohol. A much better approach is to express your feelings, get them out. Keep a journal. Confide in a friend. Have a good cry.

There will also be times when you just need to blow off steam. At those times, try losing yourself in a physical activity like exercise or doing some household chore that takes energy but little thought.

symptoms of depression

Usually when a teen says, "Oh, I'm so depressed," he or she is just sad or upset about something. It's a mood, and it will pass. How do you know if you or a friend is really depressed and in need of professional help? Check off any of the following statements that describe you or your friend:

☐ You feel deeply sad, hopeless or worthless, and you can't shake the feeling.

☐ You're no longer interested in activities you used to enjoy.

☐ You don't have the energy you used to have.

☐ You're restless and can't concentrate long enough to do the things you have to get done.

☐ You've experienced a big change in appetite: You hardly ever feel like eating, or you feel like eating all the time.

☐ You've experienced a big change in weight: You're losing or gaining without trying.

☐ You've experienced a big change in sleep patterns: You're sleepy a lot, or you have trouble sleeping.

☐ You feel terribly guilty over things that are not your fault.

☐ You have been thinking about death or suicide.

Of course there can be reasons other than depression for any of the above. But if you checked off the first or second statement plus several others, and if you've had these symptoms for two weeks or more, get help from a trained professional, such as a social worker, psychologist, therapist or counselor. Depression can be treated successfully.

Adapted from *American Psychiatric Association: Diagnostic and Statistical Manual of Mental Disorders*, Fourth Edition, Washington, D.C. 2000.

depression

Everyone feels sad and down once in a while. However, if your sad, down feelings hang on for weeks, you may be depressed. Experts say that more than 18 million Americans suffer from depression each year. Depression affects about 5% of all teens.

Depression can range from mild to very severe. At its most severe, it can make people want to run away, hurt themselves or commit suicide.

People who are depressed feel sad or hopeless or worthless or guilty. They may lose energy, lose interest in activities, lose the ability to concentrate. Changes in appetite, weight and sleeping patterns are common.

All types of depression can be treated by a health care professional, and most cases can be cured. The social worker or counselor probably will try to figure out what's causing the depression and offer help in coping with it. In some cases, medicine may be prescribed.

If you have sad, down feelings that hang on for weeks, ask for help.

Unfortunately, some depressed teens don't ask for the help they need. They may feel embarrassed, think that they'll get over it, or believe that nothing will help.

Now hear this: Getting help for depression — yours or a friend's — is vital. If you or someone you know is showing signs of depression, tell a trusted adult, counselor or health care professional. They may be able to help you see your situation in a different light or suggest solutions to your problems.

If you or someone you know is considering suicide, get help right away. Eight out of 10 people who commit suicide tell someone about it before they make the attempt. Call the National Suicide Prevention Lifeline at 1-800-273-TALK (8255) or the National Suicide Prevention Hotline at 1-800-SUICIDE (784-2433).

One way to find a local crisis center is by using the Crisis Center Locator on the National Suicide Prevention Lifeline website, www.suicidepreventionlifeline.org. It will search by state or zip code for the center nearest you.

(For more information about suicide and how to prevent it, see pages 102-103.)

stressful situations

Imagine yourself in each of the stressful situations pictured here. What could you do to reduce the stress you feel? List below three things that stress you out and what you could do to reduce the stress in each situation. Share your list with a friend and borrow each other's stress-busting ideas.

1. I feel stressed when _____

   I could reduce my stress by _____

2. I feel stressed when _____

   I could reduce my stress by _____

3. I feel stressed when _____

   I could reduce my stress by _____

stress

All of us face stresses big and small throughout our lives. The changes and challenges of the puberty years can add to your stress.

Look at the stress-causers in your life and divide them into two categories: things you can do something about and things that are beyond your control.

You might be stressed out because you forgot to study for a test, for example. You can reduce or eliminate that source of stress by asking the teacher about extra credit work and studying extra hard for future tests. You may be causing stress yourself by overloading your schedule or pushing yourself toward impossible perfection. You can try scaling back and easing up.

It is harder to deal with stress caused by things that are beyond our control, such as a parent's illness or job loss, or frightening events in the world around us. Even an event that is far away, such as an earthquake or a terrorist attack in another country, can make people feel stressed.

Learn how stress works, and you will cope with it better.

Stress is part of your natural survival kit. When faced with a stressful situation — say, the approach of a bully — your body prepares for either "fight" (attack the bully) or "flight" (run away). The hormone adrenaline (a-DREN-a-lin) temporarily makes you stronger and more alert.

In reality, you can't always use your adrenaline surge to fight the stress-causer or run away from it. When you can't put the extra adrenaline to use, it bottles up inside you, giving you tense muscles, a head-ache, stomach pain, sweat, a pounding heart, a dry mouth, cold hands, or some combination of those symptoms.

Some young people mistakenly believe that smoking cigarettes, drinking alcohol or taking drugs will relieve stress. In fact, these substances cause more problems that ultimately add to your stress level.

If there's nothing you can do to change the source of the stress, you need to find positive ways to deal with it. Physical activity helps people cope with all types of stress. So does getting your feelings out by talking with a friend or trusted adult.

ways to express feelings

There are different ways to express emotion. Some forms of expression have better results than others. For example, if you express your emotions in a way that makes you feel relief and calm — those would be good results. If you express your emotions in a way that hurts another person or breaks something, those would be bad results. Think of a time when you saw each of the emotions listed expressed by a character in a book, movie or TV show. Compare the character's reaction with your reaction to the same emotion.

Rejection
- What caused the character to feel rejected?
- How did he/she express it?
- The last time you felt rejected, what caused it?
- How did you express it?

Sadness
- What caused the character to feel sad?
- How did he/she express it?
- The last time you felt sad, what caused it?
- How did you express it?

Disappointment
- What caused the character to feel disappointed?
- How did he/she express it?
- The last time you felt disappointed, what caused it?
- How did you express it?

Remorse
- What caused the character to feel remorseful?
- How did he/she express it?
- The last time you felt remorseful, what caused it?
- How did you express it?

boys have feelings

A lot of people used to think being a man meant being strong and silent. Boys who showed their emotions were "sissies," they believed. Men, it was said, should never, ever cry.

Everyone has feelings. It's only fair that everyone be allowed to express them.

Maybe you fought with a friend. Maybe your grandfather died. Maybe you tried out for the track team and didn't make it. In each of those cases, your sadness is real.

Holding in your feelings makes the hurt worse. No matter what is causing you emotional pain, you will probably heal faster if you talk about it or write about it or express your feelings in some other way. Crying is a great way to vent sad feelings.

The young people who hide their feelings may have many more emotional problems later in their life. They may have health problems too. Many health problems are caused or made worse by stress or bottled-up emotions.

Holding in your feelings makes the hurt worse.

Imitating the macho act they see in movies and video games may also cause trouble for boys in relationships with girls. That superior, tough-guy attitude is often a shield put up by a boy who is sensitive and afraid of rejection. Girls don't have X-ray vision; they can't see through the shield. What they see turns them off.

Relationships have a better chance of working out when boyfriends and girlfriends listen to their feelings, share them, and show respect for each other.

Note: You may notice that you are better at expressing your feelings than older men you know. Because they grew up believing they shouldn't, it can be hard for them to show feelings now, even if they want to. And they may not know how to react when you express your feelings. Don't let that stop you from being expressive. They'll get used to it, and may eventually follow your lead.

your gifts, their gifts

We all have gifts and challenges, things that are easier for us and things that are more difficult.

A person's gifts might make it easier for him or her to get As in school, to excel at sports, to get the lead in the school play or the solo part in the band concert.

What are your gifts? Are you well-organized, a great listener, a terrific cook? Think about the things you are good at and list them on this page.

My gifts

_____

_____

_____

_____

_____

Now think about your challenges, the things that are more difficult for you. Do you know people for whom these things seem to come easily?

List below some things that are difficult for you, and the name of someone in your family, school or community who is especially good at it.

• This is difficult for me: _____

But it's easy for: _____

• This is difficult for me: _____

But it's easy for: _____

• This is difficult for me: _____

But it's easy for: _____

girls have brains

Experts say a strange thing sometimes happens to girls in middle and junior high school. Some smart girls who used to raise their hands and participate in class discussions suddenly become quiet. They let the boys grab all the attention. They seem to think that smart girls aren't supposed to act smart — at least, not in front of boys.

This is a serious problem and it's attracting a growing amount of concern from schools and parents.

What's the situation in your classroom? If you're a girl, do you worry that by showing you have brains you will scare away boys who might be interested in you? If you're a boy, do you lose interest in a girl if you find out she's smart, or smarter than you?

Is it true that girls who act smart scare away the boys?

Once you reach college age, these questions will probably seem silly. Most adults admire brains; they admire women as well as men who use their brains well.

During puberty, though, the questions can be very real. One reason is that boys your age are trying to figure out what it means to be a man. Boys may think, "men are bigger, stronger, and better at everything than women." To them, any girl who seems faster, stronger or better than them at anything is a threat. A boy might ignore a girl who seems a threat, or he might make fun of her by calling her names.

Girls and boys should not pretend to be less than they are. If you do that, you cheat yourself out of becoming the best person you can be.

Just wait, you'll see: most boys will eventually settle on a more mature definition of manhood — one that respects women as equals. Until then, speak up!

gaining control

A typical pessimist feels "bad things happen to me and there's nothing I can do about it."

Do you feel that way? Do you feel out of control?

To gain a more optimistic outlook on life, you have to gain control. You have to change the way you think about the bad things that happen.

On this page, compare the way optimists and pessimists think about common situations. The next time you feel out of control, come back to this page and imagine how an optimist would react in your situation.

- Your group gets a bad mark on a social studies project.

Pessimists deny responsibility.

I always get stuck in the worst group.

Optimists accept responsibility.

I could have done more to help my group succeed.

- You can't figure out your math homework.

Pessimists see small problems as part of a large problem that can't be solved.

I must be really stupid.

Optimists see small problems as small. With action, a problem can be solved.

I didn't pay attention in class today.

- You and your brother just had another fight.

Pessimists think a problem now will be a problem forever.

We're always fighting.

Optimists think a problem now might not be a problem later.

My brother is in a bad mood.

- Your birthday swim party is postponed due to bad weather.

Pessimists think life is unfair to them, so why bother trying to make it better.

Of course rain ruins my birthday.

Optimists think life is unfair to everyone, so why not make the best of it.

I hope everyone can come next Friday.

Optimism

What you think affects what you feel. If you think things are going to go badly for you, it's a good bet you feel bad most of the time. On the other hand, if you think you have a pretty good chance of being successful at things, you're likely to feel good.

We call a person who usually fears the worst a pessimist (PESS-ih-mist). A person who usually hopes for the best is called an optimist (OP-tih-mist). It's better to be an optimist because optimists not only feel better, they succeed more and have fewer health problems. In other words, a person's attitude about the future can actually affect the kind of future he or she has.

Your attitude affects your future. So have a good one.

If you tend to be a pessimist, don't despair: You can train yourself to think more optimistically. You can choose to savor your achievements rather than dwell on your failures. You can choose to look at a setback or disappointment as temporary rather than forever. You can choose to solve the parts of a problem that are under your control, instead of letting a big problem control you.

Feeling optimistic means feeling you have choices, feeling in control, feeling the future is bright.

In this booklet, you're going to learn about some of the dangers young people face that can threaten their futures. These dangers include a pregnancy that wasn't intended and harmful habits such as using drugs, drinking alcohol and smoking cigarettes — habits that often start during puberty. Also dangerous are people who abuse young teens physically, sexually or emotionally — often causing lasting harm. You're going to learn how to protect yourself from these threats, how to make good choices, stay in control, and get help if you need it.

A healthy, successful, happy future doesn't just happen. You make it happen. And you can start now. Picture the future you want and hold that picture in your head. When you have a choice to make or a problem to solve, think about how your action — or inaction — will affect your future. Think positively, and act with hope.

chapter 3

me + my friends

importance of peers

peer pressure

respecting differences

conflict

how much in common?

How much alike are you and your best friend? Here is a quiz you can take together to measure your compatibility.

1. My favorite thing to do on the weekend is:

a. go to a party

b. spend time with a small group of friends

c. be alone

d. do lots of different things

2. When I get upset, it's usually over:

a. my grades

b. my looks

c. the opposite sex

d. family problems

3. My dream vacation would be:

a. the beach

b. an African safari

c. hiking in the wilderness

d. shows and shopping in New York City

4. My favorite subject in school is:

a. English

b. History or Social Studies

c. Science

d. Math

5. If I have romantic feelings about someone, I tend to:

a. try to talk to them and show my interest

b. watch them from afar and hope

c. plan to be in the same places they are

d. ask a friend to find out if they like me

6. If I got $200 for my birthday, I would:

a. put it away for college

b. splurge on something awesome

c. enjoy spending it on a lot of small things

d. put it toward some big item that I'm saving up for

7. When there's a new fad at school, I'm usually:

a. the first to wear it or do it

b. the last to know or care

c. somewhere in the vast middle of the crowd

How did your answers compare? Do you have a lot in common? Or are you and your friend a case of opposites attracting?

importance of peers

When you were little, the most important people in the world to you were your parents. In puberty, your friends are becoming more and more important. Sometimes, you may even feel closer to your friends than to your family.

It's normal to feel that way. Part of growing up is, little by little, becoming independent from the adults who are raising you. You still love them — you just don't need them in quite the same way.

As a young child, you got your first sense of who you are from your place in the family group. That identity is with you forever. But now that you're getting older, your identity is expanding. You are searching for your place in a peer group, the group of boys and girls your age. Who you are in that group will become part of your identity — part of the way you think about yourself.

Parents are no longer at the center of your life; peers are.

It's natural to care about the way others in the peer group see you. You want to be accepted and liked. So you may find yourself dressing or talking or acting the way your peers do — even if it's different from the way people in your family dress and talk and act. These outward changes in you are just a sign of the inward shift from a family-centered life to a life that centers on peers.

Many boys and girls have a special best friend. You may spend a lot of time together, doing things you both enjoy and sharing your hopes and worries. You two may stay best friends for a lifetime — or until next week. That's normal, too. During puberty, there's so much change going on in both of you that growing apart is as likely as growing together.

If you and your friend do grow apart, keep in mind that others around you have been growing and changing, too. Maybe that boy or girl you didn't like last year will be your new best friend.

prepared for peer pressure

Think of a real situation in which you have felt peer pressure. Or imagine such a situation. Work through this exercise.

You'll be preparing yourself to deal with similar situations in the future.

• My friends want me to...

_____

• But I don't want to because...

_____

• What do I risk or lose by going along?

_____

• What do I risk or lose by resisting?

_____

• Which is less risky, going along or resisting?

_____

• If I could say to these friends what I truly feel, I would say...

_____

• Why can't I be honest with them about how I feel?

_____

• I could try a little humor or exaggeration to get me out of this
  (such as, "If I drink that, I'll throw up and it won't be a pretty sight"); I could say...

_____

• I could use the old "parents" excuse
  (such as, "My parents would ground me"); I could say...

_____

peer pressure

Has a friend ever tried to pressure you into doing something you didn't want to do? That's called peer pressure, and if it hasn't happened to you yet, it's bound to happen during your puberty years.

Peer pressure can be positive or negative. Say you've started hanging out with a bad crowd and getting into trouble. If your old friends pressure you to ditch the troublemakers and hang with them again, that's positive peer pressure.

Here are some examples of giving in to negative peer pressure:

It's a powerful force. Even adults give in some- times.

• A popular girl you want to impress asks you to help her shoplift from a store. You know it's wrong and you're afraid of getting caught. You start to say no but join in after she calls you a coward or a wuss.

• There's a new kid at school. You've met him because he moved into a house on your street. You think he's nice, but your friends say he's a weirdo, so you ignore him at school.

Peer pressure is a powerful force. It doesn't begin or end with puberty. It's something we all have to deal with. And everyone gives in to it sometimes — even adults! (Have you ever seen your parents buy something they really couldn't afford just because their friends have one?)

Here are a few tactics for handling peer pressure:

• Don't put yourself in situations where you have to make an on-the-spot decision. If you know the kids are going somewhere to do things you don't want to do, don't go with them.

• Express your feelings honestly. People usually respect someone who speaks up to say, "I don't feel good about this."

• Say a flat "no." Don't be trapped into having to give reasons and defend them.

exploring differences

In each box below, sketch one person who fits the category. Then write several ways in which this person is the same as you and several ways in which he or she is different.

Person in my neighborhood

Name _____

Ways we are the same _____

_____

Ways we are different _____

_____

Person in my school

Name _____

Ways we are the same _____

_____

Ways we are different _____

_____

Person in the news

Name _____

Ways we are the same _____

_____

Ways we are different _____

_____

respecting differences

When you move from an elementary school to a middle or junior high school, your world is suddenly a lot bigger. As you grow up, you'll realize more and more that we live in a huge and varied world where many people don't look like you, talk like you, dress like you or think like you.

Some people's skin is a different color from yours. Other people follow a different religion or speak a different language. Some have more money than your family, or less. Some are gay or lesbian. Some have extraordinary abilities, some have different abilities, and some have disabilities.

Respecting differences means showing respect for people who have different ways of thinking, acting, talking, dressing or worshipping.

Some people can't accept differences. They make fun or say mean things about people who are not like them. They may be prejudiced against a racial, religious or ethnic group because they hear hateful remarks about the group from relatives or neighbors. They may see that a few people in a group have done something horrible and they react with prejudice against everyone in the group. For example, after a small number of terrorists attacked the U.S. on 9/11/2001, there was prejudice against millions of people who are Arab or Muslim.

All people in your life won't be like you. You might like them.

Think about it: Do you deserve to be blamed for bad things done by people who share your ethnic background or religion? How would you feel if you were blamed?

Your life will be much more interesting if you make friends among a great variety of people. You can start now. Think of someone you haven't gotten to know because he or she seemed different. Next time you see that person, smile and say, "Hi." If you two can start a conversation, you may be surprised at what you have in common.

What can you do when others say cruel, prejudiced things? Silence makes it look like you agree, while lecturing them about prejudice can make you an outcast. Instead, play dumb. Say, "I don't get that joke," or "What do you mean?" The more they keep talking and explaining, the dumber they'll sound.

47

come up with a compromise

The cartoons on this page show conflict situations. Look at each one and write your suggestion for a compromise in which each person gives up something so that both can walk away as winners.

Compromise _____

_____

_____

_____

Compromise _____

_____

_____

_____

Compromise _____

_____

_____

_____

conflict

No matter how hard you try, you will never convince everyone else in your life to do everything your way. So conflict is a part of life. A conflict is not a fight, although it can become one. A conflict is any situation in which what you want and what someone else wants are different.

Learning to "work it out" rather than "fight it out" can help you avoid frustration and hurt feelings. In a fight, someone wins and someone loses. When you work it out, you both win.

In schools across the country, students are learning how to solve problems through something called conflict resolution. When two students argue about something, a third student trained as a mediator (MEE-dee-ay-tor) — someone who helps to work out differences — helps guide them to a peaceful solution. Mediator training involves listening carefully, staying calm and helping people communicate better.

Why fight it out, and risk losing, when you can work it out and win?

The next time you have a conflict with another person, it might turn out better if you:

• Find a place to talk that is away from other people and distractions.

• Look the other person in the eye. Eye contact sends a message that you are being sincere and honest.

• Don't accuse the other person. Instead, describe your feelings clearly. Start sentences with "I feel..." instead of "You always..."

• When the other person talks, think about what he or she is saying and don't interrupt. To show that you're listening and trying to understand, repeat what you think the person said.

• If you can't agree or even compromise, then agree to disagree.

Note: If you're ever in a conflict where violence is a possibility, don't try to resolve it alone. Seek help from an adult you trust. If you are threatened with a weapon, let the person "win" the conflict, walk away, and report the incident to an adult immediately.

chapter 4

me + my sexuality

sexual feelings
love and lust
sexual expression
masturbation
sexual intercourse
deciding about sex
pressure to have sex
oral sex, anal sex
how far is too far?
birth control
emergency contraception
pregnancy
options in pregnancy
STDs
HIV + AIDS

dealing with feelings

How do you let a special person know you like him or her? What do you do if someone likes you and you're not interested in that person? What if no one seems interested in you?

These are some of the new issues that come up after you start having sexual feelings. And by the way, after these feelings start you can't stop them. So you have to deal with the issues.

A popular way to do that is by talking with close friends your own age. But it can really help to have a trusted adult to confide in as well: a family member, your health care provider, minister, priest or rabbi, a counselor at a family planning clinic.

The hardest part about discussing romance with an adult can be knowing how to start. You'd probably be embarrassed to say, "Mom, can we talk about my sexual feelings?" Here are some questions you could use as conversation-starters:

- How old were you when you had your first boyfriend or girlfriend?

- What was your first date like?

- Who was the first boy/girl you ever kissed?

- How did you know when you really fell in love?

- What do you wish someone had told you about dating so that you wouldn't have had to learn it the hard way?

What other questions can you think of that might get you started talking with an adult about romance? Write them down:

_____

_____

Once you get the conversation rolling, what do you really want to know? Write down your most urgent questions:

_____

_____

sexual feelings

During puberty, you'll probably begin to feel interested in your own body and other people's bodies. You may get romantic feelings about another boy or girl at school, a movie star or even a teacher. You may daydream about being close to that special someone. You may get the urge to touch yourself to get sexual pleasure (for more on masturbation, turn to page 59).

There's nothing wrong with you if you have these kinds of sexual or romantic feelings. And there's nothing wrong with you if you don't yet. Remember, everyone goes through puberty at a different speed. If a boy or girl you like in that special way isn't responding, don't assume he or she doesn't like you. That boy or girl might be unable to respond — his or her sexual feelings switch hasn't turned on yet.

Starting to have sexual feelings is an exciting part of growing up. You might look at someone who has been a classmate for years, then suddenly find yourself staring and thinking "wow." You might feel happy about your new feelings, or scared, or both. You might become shy around a childhood friend because now your heart flutters whenever he or she smiles. You might be confused by those feelings, or embarrassed — but instead of wanting those feelings to stop, you want to see your friend smile again.

There's nothing wrong with having lots of sexual feelings, or none.

Sexual feelings waken you to the possibility of a new type of relationship in your life: a romantic relationship. At some point you will want to act on your feelings and explore that kind of relationship. You'll want to have a boyfriend or girlfriend. That's when you'll find out just how complicated — how absolutely wonderful and heart-breakingly awful — a romantic relationship can be.

Note: Some boys have sexual feelings for boys and some girls for girls. Some of these boys and girls grow up to be homosexual (gay or lesbian), some don't. Some grow up to be bisexual, which means they have sexual feelings for both boys and girls. Sexual feelings can take years to sort out.

loves me, loves me not

When you're going through puberty it's hard enough to sort out your own feelings for other people. How can you really know what another person feels for you?

This question becomes important when you are attracted to someone special. You want to know if that person is attracted to you as a whole person, or only as a face and body that might be fun to fool around with.

You can't always know right away, but you'll guess right most of the time if you look for messages in the person's actions rather than in his or her words.

Some people can say "I love you" and not mean it. Others may truly feel love and not be able to get the words out. In both cases, their actions will tell you the truth.

To explore this idea, look at the actions in the flower petals on this page. Circle the kind, unselfish actions that say "loves me" and cross out the unkind, selfish actions that say "loves me not."

Writes an original poem or song dedicated to you.

Embarrasses you by telling others about things you say or do in private.

Forgets to call at the time you said you were free to talk.

Listens when you want to talk about something that's important to you.

Invites you to join in whenever friends are getting together.

Calls you when you're home sick from school just to make you feel better.

Agrees to meet up with you and arrives late or doesn't show up at all.

Keeps touching you after you say to stop.

Waits at your locker every morning just to see you for a few minutes before class starts.

Makes your favorite cake for you on your birthday.

love and lust

Lust is a sexual feeling. It is physical attraction, the intense desire to touch, hug and kiss a special person. When two people lust for each other we call it "chemistry," and there's some scientific evidence that physical attraction actually is linked to a chemical reaction in your body.

Two people may feel that kind of mutual passion the first time they meet. "It was love at first sight," they'll say.

Well, maybe and maybe not. Is love a sexual feeling? Partly, yes. The way you love your mother or your best friend is not sexual. But the tingles you feel when you're "in love" with an attractive boy or girl are sexual tingles — eager, exciting tingles.

How do you know if you are truly in love?

So how do you know if you're truly in love, or just "in lust"?

Many philosophers, poets and songwriters have tried to define love. They can describe its elements: strong affection, unselfish concern, warm attachment. But they can't define it, because among love's many wonders is this: Love is both universal — felt by everyone, and unique — felt by each of us in a different way.

One thing is for sure: When you fall in love for the first time it is a magical experience. You have new feelings you can't explain. You feel good, full of energy and purpose. By returning your love with kindness and caring, he or she makes you feel like the luckiest person on earth.

You want those feelings to go on forever, but they don't. Both of you fell in love with someone you hardly knew. He or she seemed perfect at first because, knowing very little about this person, you could "fill in the blanks" with your imagination. Over time, as you get to know this real person, you may find that he or she is not as perfect as you imagined.

True love is lasting. It is a commitment to the beloved "as is."

showing you care

"Doing it" isn't the only way to show someone that you care. List as many ideas as you can to express intimate romantic feelings to someone special.

- Give or welcome a hug

- Give or return a kiss

- Give or accept a ring

- Hold hands

- Walk arm in arm

- "Friend" each other on a social website, like Facebook

- Talk on the phone

- Text each other silly messages

- Become instant messaging buddies

- Give comfort when the other is sad

- Share your hopes and dreams

- Snuggle up, cuddle and nuzzle

- Take a picnic lunch to a pretty place

- Cook the other person's favorite dish

- Bake cookies together

- Shop for and prepare a meal together

- Share a candlelight dinner

- Do your homework together

- Host a party together

- Gaze into each other's eyes

- Do volunteer work together

- Choose a special love song

- Dedicate a song on the radio

- Record a CD of love songs

- Make popcorn and watch a DVD together

- Read the same book and share your thoughts and feelings about it

- Go to the park at sunset

- Try a new sport or activity together

- Trust each other with secrets

- Meet each other's families

- Send a funny card

- Hide a love note where the other will find it

- Write a love poem

- Make a special gift

- Present a bouquet of wildflowers

- Call each other by pet names

- Do favors without being asked

- Whisper into the other's ear

- Be loyal

- Stick up for each other

sexual expression

Two people may express sexual, romantic or loving feelings in many ways. They may hold hands. Or kiss. Or cuddle. Or dance together. As a relationship progresses, the couple may touch each other's sexual parts.

Note: A person your age has a lot to think about before expressing sexual feelings by having sexual intercourse, which is when a male puts his erect penis inside the female's vagina. You'll see why in the pages that follow.

How you express your sexual feelings will have a lot to do with your values. Your family, culture or religion may have customs or rules about sexual expression that you want to observe. If you don't understand them, you need to ask the adults in your family.

You can express your sexual feelings toward another in many ways.

Below are some terms you may hear when people talk about sexual expression. Keep in mind that for each activity described, some people enjoy it and others don't. Ask your partner "Is this okay?" before engaging in any form of sexual activity. Respect you partner's right to say no, or to stop if he or she suddenly feels uncomfortable.

• *French kissing* is when one or both people use their tongues while kissing.

• *Petting* means touching or rubbing the other person's breasts or genitals. Petting can progress from touching over clothing to touching under clothing.

• *Making out* is kissing for a long time, possibly petting as well.

• *Oral sex* is when one or both people use their mouths to stimulate the other's genitals. (More about oral sex on page 67.)

• *Anal sex* is when the penis penetrates the anus. (More about anal sex on page 67.)

• *Doing everything but* means the two people don't have intercourse but they may take off some or all clothing, touch each other and be close in other ways.

• *Going all the way* often means sexual intercourse in which the penis penetrates the vagina. (More about sexual intercourse on page 61.)

Remember: Don't do anything that doesn't feel right for you.

masturbation myths

A few generations ago, many people believed that horrible things happened to people who masturbated. There were myths that masturbation could:

• make warts grow on your nose

• make hair grow on the palms of your hands

• cause pimples

• cause blindness

• soften your brain

• make you go insane

If those myths were true, there would have been a lot of warty, hairy, pimply, blind, insane people walking around!

Today, some kids worry that masturbating too much will hurt their sex organs, but there's really little cause for concern. If you rub your genitals a lot, they could get a little sore, but there would be no lasting harm.

masturbation

Some people find an outlet for sexual feelings through masturbation (mass-ter-BAY-shun). When you masturbate, you stroke, rub or squeeze your most sensitive sex organs: your penis if you are a boy, your clitoris if you are a girl. You are giving yourself sexual pleasure. If you choose to masturbate, it is something to do in private.

Some people masturbate often when they are alone, some once in awhile, others never. Some people have sexual daydreams or a fantasy when they masturbate. They think about an experience that is sexually exciting. Like a dream, it may involve real or imagined people and places, or a combination.

Your family may have religious or cultural reasons for frowning on masturbation. The important thing to remember is, masturbating or "playing with yourself" won't injure you.

Most babies and little children masturbate, but they don't realize what they're doing. They explore their bodies all over, and enjoy touching places that feel particularly good.

If you masturbate, you may begin to feel warm and tingly and excited all through your body. As you continue, you may build up to a very intense moment called an orgasm (OR-gaz-em). At that moment, you will feel strong pulsing or throbbing sensations; in your penis if you are a boy, in the area around your vulva if you are a girl. The pleasurable sensations may spread around your whole body. Afterward, you may feel relaxed and satisfied.

You can give yourself sexual pleasure. It won't harm you.

Having an orgasm is also called "cuming" or reaching "climax." During orgasm, a boy will ejaculate (ee-JACK-you-late), spurting a milky liquid called semen (SEE-men) from his penis. A girl may feel some wetness seeping from her vagina.

Boys seem to talk about masturbation more than girls. They use many slang terms for it, including "jerking off" and "beating off."

before you have sex

If you think you might be ready to have sexual intercourse, weigh the pros and cons. Ask yourself, what good things may result if I do this, and what bad things might result? Then change the "I" to "we" and ask your partner.

You can walk yourself through the pros and cons talk by writing responses to the three questions below.

If you want to have intercourse but don't want to make a baby, you must choose either to abstain (not do it) or to use birth control (see page 71). Couples also need to decide how they will protect themselves from getting sexually transmitted diseases and HIV (see pages 78-81).

1. "I love you and I want to make love. Can you think of any reason for us not to?"

_____

2. "I can think of lots of good things that might happen if we do it. You can too, right?"

_____

3. "If we're careful, don't you think we can have the good things and avoid the bad?"

_____

sexual intercourse

Sexual expression becomes sexual intercourse when the male puts his erect penis inside the female's vagina. He may be lying on top of her, or she on top of him; the two can be sitting face to face, kneeling — couples experiment with different positions.

A person who hasn't had sexual intercourse is a "virgin."

As the male and female move their hips back and forth in rhythm, the rubbing together of their sensitive sex organs can give both of them pleasure. The two may hug, kiss and stroke each other's bodies; they might also whisper or make sounds.

When the male reaches the peak of his sexual excitement, he will ejaculate, spurting semen (SEE-men) from his penis into the female's vagina. Swimming in the semen are millions of tiny sperm. The sperm make their way up the vagina, through the cervix, and into the uterus. (To review these body parts, see pages 2-5.) If a sperm finds an egg in the Fallopian tube and unites with it, the female will become pregnant.

If you're not ready yet, sex can be painful instead of pleasurable.

Many people think of sexual intercourse as "making love," a very intimate experience between two people who want to share everything — even their most private selves.

But intercourse can also be painful to the bodies and emotions of people who aren't really ready for it. A male may be too rough or too rushed to make intercourse pleasurable for a female. One or both partners may lack the maturity to handle the strong emotions that come with giving to someone else parts of themselves that have always been private.

Emotional pain is almost certain if one partner is "making love" while the other is only "having sex," satisfying a lustful urge that has nothing to do with feelings for the partner. Some people think there's nothing bad about having sex just for fun, without emotional attachment. Your opinion about that might come from your family's values, religion or culture. But no matter what your opinion, you're going to feel used if you give yourself to someone you care about before finding out if they care for you as well.

clear-headed thinking

You make lots of little decisions every day: what to wear, what to eat for lunch, what book to choose from the library.

Sometimes you make decisions that are bigger because the results will be more long-lasting; for example, what color to paint your bedroom.

You decide more carefully if it's a big decision because you know you'll have to live with the results. Decisions about your sexual behavior are very big. They affect how you feel about yourself and how others feel about you.

Some of the issues you might have to face when deciding about sex are listed on this page. Think clearly and check the box that shows your answer.

If you need more information or advice before answering, ask an adult you trust. You could even ask that adult to check the boxes for his or her answers and explain them.

A = Important reason _not_ to go ahead with sexual behavior.

B = Important reason to go ahead with sexual behavior.

C = Not important to me; wouldn't matter either way.

A B C

☐ ☐ ☐ My family or religion tells me not to do this.

☐ ☐ ☐ The laws in my state make it illegal for someone my age to have sex.*

☐ ☐ ☐ I'm curious about what this is like, and if I don't do this now, I may not get another opportunity for awhile.

☐ ☐ ☐ I might like this, but I'm afraid I won't like it and then be too embarrassed to say I don't want to do this anymore.

☐ ☐ ☐ My friend told me he/she did this and it was _gross_.

☐ ☐ ☐ My friend told me he/she did this and it was _great_.

☐ ☐ ☐ If my boyfriend/girlfriend tells others I did this, I will get a bad reputation as "fast," "easy" or "slut."

☐ ☐ ☐ If my boyfriend/girlfriend tells others I did this, people will be impressed with me.

* _Note: In some states it is against the law for young teenagers to have sex with a person who is older. If you are worried about this, ask your healthcare provider._

deciding about sex

Deciding what you will or won't do sexually may be among the toughest decisions you've faced in your life so far. Sexual impulses can be very strong and confusing. It's easy to get swept up in a rush of tingling feelings.

For example, a boy may know he's not ready for intercourse but find himself involved with a girl who is experienced and eager. Afraid she'll make fun of him for being a virgin (someone who has never had intercourse), he may convince himself he has to have sex to prove his manhood. A girl may have told herself, "I'll kiss him, but no petting." Then the kissing gets intense, she goes with the flow and regrets it later.

To avoid those "wish I hadn't" situations, do some clear-headed, unemotional thinking about sex before you get yourself in a sexual situation — where thinking gets messed up and emotions are in high gear.

You want to avoid those "wish I hadn't" situations.

Keep your thinking clear by steering away from alcohol and drugs, which can cause you to do things you wouldn't do sober. Be especially careful to avoid "date rape drugs" such as "roofies" (Rohypnol). When slipped into a drink, these drugs cause sleepiness, confusion, loss of self control and amnesia. To protect yourself at parties and dances, keep your drink near you and hang with your friends.

If you get into a sexual situation — whether on purpose or by mistake — don't feel you've given up your right to stop it. You can always say "no" at any time, and so can your boyfriend or girlfriend. To protect each other from hurt feelings, try saying what your limits are before the kissing begins.

If you believe what you see on TV or in movies, you might think that sex happens very quickly when two people are attracted. In fact, real-life romantic relationships usually go through several stages first — and many relationships end before intercourse. How far you go, and how fast, is up to you.

<u>Do</u> what feels right *for you*. <u>Don't</u> have sex if you don't really want to, or have sex with a stranger, or have sex even once without a condom. You risk your health, and maybe your life (see pages 74-81). You also may risk breaking the law. In some states it is illegal for young teenagers to have sex with a person who is older. If you are worried about this, ask your healthcare provider.

63

saying no nicely

People get all emotional about sex. Should I? Shouldn't I? Will she? Won't he? If you're the one asking, you're afraid of being rejected. If you're the one being asked, you're afraid of being rejected for saying no.

My partner wants to, but I don't

If a person you didn't care about asked you to have sex, it would be easy to say no. But that is rarely the case. Pressure to have sex usually comes from someone you care about very much—a person who says he or she also cares about you.

If you're like most people, you want to please those you care about and you want to avoid hurting their feelings. This can make it hard to refuse a request, especially a plea that comes packaged in pretty words like "I love you."

But if you want to say no, then you owe it to yourself to say no. If you give in, someone's feelings will still be hurt—only that someone will be you!

I want to, but my partner doesn't

If you feel ready to have sex and you want to ask your partner, be prepared to hear a no. Even if your partner cares for you and finds you attractive and desirable, he or she may not want to be that intimate with you.

There are many good reasons a person who has feelings for you may refuse to have sex with you. Your partner might have moral objections based on religious or family standards, might want to know you better first, or might feel he or she is too young. Or your partner may say no without being able to say why—he or she is just unsure or uncomfortable.

Try to accept a no without feeling rejected. "It's not you" is probably true!

You can find a way to say no nicely. Role-play some of the suggested responses below, then come up with some of your own. Ask friends you trust how they would feel if their partner said no in these words. Share ideas for other ways to say no.

"If I were going to have sex, I would want it to be with you, but I've decided to wait."

"I love you, too, but I'm just not ready."

"You know I have feelings for you, but this doesn't feel right."

"I think you're very cute, but I don't know you well enough."

"I do trust you, but I'm uncomfortable with it."

"That might be fun sometime, but let's try other ways of being close first."

pressure to have sex

Nearly every teen will experience pressure to "go all the way" at some point. Putting this kind of pressure on another person is just plain wrong. And it is selfish. Someone who pressures you to have sexual intercourse before you're ready is *not* thinking about what's best for you.

You may hear pressure lines like, "If you loved me you would." That's one of the classics — it's been around for centuries. You may even be afraid your boyfriend or girlfriend will leave you if you don't give in. If someone really cares for you, he or she won't leave just because you say no. If your partner does leave, that's a sign that he or she didn't really care about you. Plenty of people will like you even if you don't have sex with them.

There are a lot of good reasons teens choose to abstain from intercourse. Abstinence (AB-stin-ence) is one sure way to take charge of your body... and your future! When you don't have sexual intercourse, you don't have to worry about pregnancy or feeling used... or getting a sexually transmitted disease.

Putting pressure on a partner to have sex is selfish.

If you decide on abstinence, how do you tell the people you date? Don't wait until you've been making out for hours to spring the news. Talk about it when you're both relaxed. Explain your feelings, values and needs. Then listen to the response.

Sometimes it may seem hard to stick with your decision. Make things easier on yourself by avoiding situations where you're likely to face sexual pressures. For example, you know that alcohol and drugs can alter your judgment. So avoid them. Double date with friends who aren't drinking or doing drugs or having sex either.

Note: You may decide to have intercourse and afterward feel it was the wrong decision for you. You can decide not to do it again. Having sex once —or even dozens of times — doesn't mean you must continue having it with that partner or with any future boyfriend or girlfriend. Pressure to continue is just as wrong as pressure to start.

dealing with pressure

If you decide to have oral or anal sex, make sure you're doing it because you want to, because it's right *for you*—not because you feel pressured. Touching another person in a way that gives sexual pleasure is a gift, and it should be given freely or not at all.

Okay, so what if you're a wimp when it comes to handling pressure? What if you really don't want to do *whatever*, because you feel it's gross, or it's humili-ating, or you just won't feel okay about it tomorrow—but you are too scared to say no?

Pressure can be tough, but even wimps can learn to handle it. All it takes is practice. Get a friend to role play with and have him/her say the pressure lines on this page while you read the responses out loud. Listen to yourself sounding sure and proud. Feel the power! You *can* do it.

"You want to as much as I do."

"No, I really don't."

"Aren't you curious what it's like?"

"I've got plenty of time to find out."

"If you won't, I'll find someone who will."

"I guess you better start looking."

"You haven't done it yet?!"

"I'll do it when I'm ready — with the right person at the right time."

"Everybody's doing it."

"I'm not everybody, and anyway, everybody isn't."

EVERYBODY

SELECT ONE:
☐ YES ☐ NO

'If you loved me, you'd do it."

'If you loved me, you wouldn't push."

⊘ral sex, anal sex

Oral sex and anal sex are ways people can express themselves sexually, whether they are heterosexual (straight), or homosexual (gay or lesbian). Regardless of sexual orientation, some people like one or both of these sexual activities and some don't.

Oral sex is kissing, licking or sucking another person's genitals to give them pleasure. In proper terms, oral contact with the male genitals is called fellatio (fell-A-she-oh) and oral contact with the female genitals is called cunnilingus (KUN-uh-lin-gus). But more often you hear slang terms such as giving head, going down, eating and blow job.

Anal sex can involve stimulating the anus with fingers, penis (anal intercourse) or mouth (proper term: analingus, slang term: rimming).

One reason young people may be attracted to oral or anal sex is that a girl doesn't risk getting pregnant.

However, both partners risk getting a sexually transmitted disease (STDs, page 79) such as herpes, syphilis or HIV. Use a condom to cover the boy's penis to protect yourself and your partner. The person receiving anal sex without a condom is at greatest risk for HIV and other STDs.

It can't cause pregnancy but it does have risks.

The other important risk to consider is emotional. Any sexual act done for the wrong reasons can make you feel bad or used. The decision to have oral or anal sex should be made carefully, just like the decision to have intercourse. It should never be made under pressure. Think about the reasons you want to touch your partner this way or let your partner touch you. It may help to go through the "before you have sex" activity on page 60 and the "clear-headed thinking" activity on page 62.

When making your decision, you also may want to consider whether your family, religion or culture approves of oral or anal sex. Some don't.

As with any other sexual activity, do only what you feel is right and comfortable — for you — and always do it safely, with a condom.

next day feelings

So, how far should you go? It depends. You need to weigh the importance to you of your friends' opinions and the values of your family and religion. You need to be honest with yourself about the relationship you're in. Do you know your partner well, care about him or her and feel sure that he or she really cares about you?

At each step in your sexual journey you need to check in with your heart to be sure that you are saying yes freely, that you are deep-down comfortable with what you're doing, that it feels right. The words below describe many different ways you *could* feel about sexual activity the next day, when you are alone and looking in the mirror. First, put a check mark next to the words that describe the way you would *like* to feel. Then put an X next to the words that describe feelings you want to avoid.

☐ I feel closer to my partner than I've ever felt before

☐ I feel I don't know my partner as well as I thought I did

☐ I feel loved

☐ I feel used

☐ I feel I used my partner

☐ I feel confused

☐ I feel I gained something

☐ I feel I lost something

☐ I feel cherished

☐ I feel abused

☐ I feel I shared a wonderful experience

☐ I feel ashamed

☐ I feel special

☐ I feel lonely

☐ I feel happy

☐ I feel sad

☐ I feel proud

☐ I feel embarrassed

☐ I feel cared for

☐ I feel neglected

☐ I feel excited about seeing my partner again

☐ I feel worried about seeing my partner again

If your X marks any feelings you've actually had after a sexual activity, you need to start saying no. It doesn't make sense to keep on doing something that makes you feel badly about yourself or your partner. You also need to forgive yourself for your mistake. You were trying something new and you didn't know how you would feel afterward. At these times it can be very useful to talk with a trusted adult who can help you deal with your feelings and decide how to handle similar situations in the future.

how far is too far?

Did you ever hear one teen asking another, "How far did you go?" and know they weren't measuring the journey in miles? They were talking about sexual behavior, right? And they were talking about it as if each kind of sexual behavior were a step toward "going all the way."

By talking this way, teens are trying to get a sense of the sexual boundaries that are accepted within their group of friends. They're trying to find out which behaviors are okay and which cross the line that gets them labeled as a "player," a "slut" or something else they don't want to be. Most teens are sensitive to the boundaries of accepted behavior within their families too. They may also want to follow the teachings of their religion.

As you mature and your sexual feelings become impossible to ignore, your need to know what is okay becomes more urgent. Because virginity is a very big deal in many cultures, and "losing" one's virginity is a very big step, teens are especially anxious to know how they can express themselves sexually without crossing the virgin line.

True or false: If you're having oral sex, you're "having sex"?

There's no easy answer. Some people define sexual relations very narrowly. To them, only vaginal intercourse is truly "having sex," and regardless of the other intimate acts they might take part in, they remain "technically" a virgin if the penis never enters the vagina. But many other people would agree that partners who are having oral sex or anal sex are "having sex." To them, those acts are every bit as intimate as intercourse — maybe more!

If you do choose to participate in intimate sexual acts, be aware that you are taking emotional and physical risks. Be smart enough to try to minimize those risks. Emotionally, the best protection is to take it slow. If you let your sexual behavior intensify gradually, one step at a time, you give yourself time between steps to think about how you feel and to see how your partner is handling your new level of intimacy. Physically, be really cautious about protecting yourself from STDs. Only vaginal sex can cause pregnancy, but STDs—including HIV—can be spread just as easily through oral or anal sex. (More on STDs and HIV on pages 78-81.)

birth control methods

<u>Notes:</u> Couples who have intercourse without any form of birth control have a nearly 85% chance of causing an unintended pregnancy within one year. **The only birth control method that also offers good protection against STDs is the condom**; contraceptive creams and foams used with a diaphragm offer some STD protection. New birth control methods are being developed, so visit www.familyplanning.org for the latest information.

DON'T WORRY, BE HAPPY YOU'RE PROTECTED

The following birth control methods are **VERY EFFECTIVE** — preventing 95% to more than 99% of possible pregnancies. **The only 100% effective way to prevent unintended pregnancy is abstinence:** not having intercourse.

- **Sterilization:** surgical procedure to make a person unable to have children (usually permanent).
- **Depo-Provera®:** Shot (injection) given in female's arm or buttocks every 3 months.
- **Patch (Ortho Evra®):** Skin patch worn on female's body. New patch applied weekly for 3 weeks; 4th week she menstruates.
- **Vaginal Ring (NuvaRing®):** Flexible ring inserted into vagina. After 3 weeks, ring is removed for a week to allow menstruation.
- **Intrauterine Device (IUD):** Small plastic device inserted into the uterus by a health care provider. Lasts from 5 to 10 years.
- **Birth Control Pill:** Pills taken every day by female.
- **Hormanal Implants (Implanon):** Tubular device about the size of a match inserted just underneath the skin; lasts three years

---

BE CAREFUL TO USE PROPERLY EVERY TIME

The following birth control methods are **SOMEWHAT EFFECTIVE** in preventing unintended pregnancy. Condoms and diaphragms are more effective when used together with a vaginal spermicide.

- **Condoms:** Male condom covers the penis and stops sperm from going into the vagina; also protects against STDs. Female condom covers the cervix, vagina and labia to stop sperm from entering.
- **Cervical Devices (Diaphragm, Lea's Shield®, FemCap®):** Covers the cervix to stop sperm from entering.
- **Vaginal spermicide:** Gel, foam, cream, film, suppository or tablet inserted into vagina to destroy sperm.

BE READY TO HANDLE A PREGNANCY

The following birth control methods are **NOT AS EFFECTIVE**.

- **Natural (Rhythm) Method:** Female refrains from intercourse during times in her cycle when pregacy is more likely.
- **Withdrawal:** Male takes penis from vagina before ejaculation.

birth control

The only 100 percent sure way to prevent pregnancy is not to have sexual intercourse. That's called abstinence (AB-stin-ence). It comes from the word abstain. When you abstain from something, you choose not to do it.

If you are going to "do it" — that is, have vaginal intercourse — and you don't want to make a baby, you must use birth control. This statistic should convince you: Four out of every five girls who don't use birth control get pregnant during the first year of sex. Some people have oral or anal sex (see page 67) to avoid causing a pregnancy, but these activities can put you at greater risk for HIV and STDs (see pages 78-81).

Birth control is anything done to prevent pregnancy. The things that are used to prevent pregnancy are called contraceptives (con-trah-SEP-tivs). There are many kinds (see page 70). Some work better than others; some are more convenient or less expensive. Some methods require a prescription from a health care provider; you can buy others (condoms, spermicides) at a drug store without a prescription.

No contraceptive is perfect. The important thing is to choose one that you can use correctly, and will use every time you have sex.

Some methods of birth control work better than others.

Getting birth control can be embarrassing. Using it can seem inconvenient or unromantic. But think: If you don't get it and use it, you're likely to cause an unintended pregnancy. How embarrassing will that be? How inconvenient?

Your town or city probably has one or more clinics that provide birth control to teens for free or at affordable prices. Both boys and girls can visit the clinic for information about birth control. The services are confidential; you don't need to have a parent's permission.

Many health facilities operate clinics. To find the clinic nearest you, visit **www.familyplanning.org**.

I won't get pregnant if I...

When a teen wakes up to the fact that he or she just had unprotected sex, the usual reaction goes something like this:

"Oh, #%*@! What if we got pregnant!?!"

Nearly 85% of girls who are having unprotected sex *do* get pregnant within one year. Desperate to believe that they are in the lucky 15 percent, teens may grab on to one of the myths about pregnancy prevention that have been passed around for years:

Myth: She won't get pregnant if she jumps up and down after sex.

Myth: She won't get pregnant if she douches (rinses out the vagina) with soda after sex.

Myth: She won't get pregnant if <u>she</u> didn't have an orgasm during sex.

Myth: She won't get pregnant if <u>he</u> didn't have an orgasm during sex.

Myth: She won't get pregnant if he withdrew his penis before ejaculating.

Myth: She won't get pregnant because you've had unprotected sex before and everything was fine so it's probably fine this time too.

<u>Reality check:</u> You *can* get pregnant if you jump up and down, douche, don't climax and do withdraw. If you've been lucky so far without protection, your luck *will* run out.
To avoid pregnancy, either don't have sex or use protection *every time* you have sex.

emergency contraception

If you do decide to have vaginal intercourse, remember that accidents can happen with any form of birth control. Possible accidents include:

- the condom breaks or slips off
- the girl forgets to take a birth control pill
- the diaphragm slips out of place
- no birth control method was used.

If an accident happens, you might want to consider emergency contraception. This is a birth control method that can be used after unprotected sex.

Emergency contraceptive pills — also called ECPs and "morning-after pills." ECPs should be taken within 72 hours (up to three days) after the accident. The sooner the pills are taken after unprotected sex, the better they work. Different types are available. Talk to a health care provider to find the one right for you.

ECPs will *not* work if you are already pregnant, so they *do not* cause an abortion. ECPs can delay or prevent ovulation, prevent fertilization of an egg, stop the egg from getting to the uterus or prevent the egg from implanting in the lining of the uterus.

"Morning-after" pills can prevent pregnancy when an accident occurs.

ECPs do not work as well as other birth control methods — so don't rely on them as your usual form of contraception. There is no guarantee that using an ECP will prevent pregnancy. ECPs also do not prevent sexually transmitted diseases such as HIV, chlamydia or herpes. (A condom is your best protection against these diseases.)

Like birth control pills, ECPs are drugs. ECPs are sold in drug stores without a prescription to people 17 and older. Teens under 17 can get ECPs with a prescription from a health care provider. ECPs can be prescribed *before* you have sex, so you can have the pills on hand if an accident occurs. For more about ECPs, go to www.not-2-late.com (The Emergency Contraception Website).

To find out where you can get emergency contraception, call 1-888-NOT-2-LATE. If you're in the Philadelphia area, you can call the CHOICE hotline at 215-985-3300.

pregnancy Q + A

Q. Could a girl get pregnant the first time she has sex?

A. Yes, it happens. A girl having sex for the first time is no more and no less likely to become pregnant than a girl who's having sex for the 50th time. A pregnancy is most likely when sex takes place during ovulation (page 75).

Q. Can a girl get pregnant if she has sex during her menstrual period?

A. Yes, although it's unusual. Since sperm can stay alive inside the girl for several days, a girl could become pregnant days after intercourse when the egg is released from the ovary into the fallopian tube.

Q. Can a girl get pregnant without having sexual intercourse?

A. It's possible. If a boy ejaculated near the opening of a girl's vagina, the sperm could swim into the vagina, into the uterus and into the fallopian tube to fertilize an egg.

Q. What if the boy takes his penis out of the girl's vagina before he ejaculates — called withdrawal or pulling out — would that prevent pregnancy?

A. No. As a male's penis gets erect, a few drops of semen often appear at the end of the penis. The fluid may contain some sperm. It only takes one sperm to start a pregnancy.

Q. Is it possible to get pregnant before having your first period?

A. It's rare but possible, because ovulation occurs before menstruation.

Q. Is there any way for a girl to get pregnant except by having a boy put his penis in her vagina or at the vagina opening?

A. No. There are many false stories about girls becoming pregnant in mysterious ways. These stories come from the imaginations of pregnant girls who are afraid to admit they were intimate with a boy. A girl can't get pregnant from kissing, sitting on a boy's lap, sitting on a toilet seat, or swimming in a pool.

"I don't know how it happened. I haven't been with any boys."

A girl can get pregnant only at a certain time of the month, during ovulation (AHV-u-lay-shun). This is when the egg, also called an ovum, has left the ovary and is traveling down the fallopian tubes to the uterus. (To review these body parts, see page 4.) Ovulation lasts 36 to 48 hours. If sperm is present during that time, it is likely that the egg and sperm will unite and a pregnancy will begin.

During ovulation the female is said to be fertile (FUR-tl). It is impossible to predict exactly when the fertile 36 to 48 hours will occur. Some women try to predict by taking their temperature daily; it rises during the fertile time. They may try to predict because they are ready to raise a child and want to become pregnant. Or they may try to predict so they can avoid having intercourse at that time (see Natural or Rhythm birth control on page 70).

Note: It is common for teenage girls to have irregular menstrual cycles. And sperm can live inside a female's body for up to five days. So anyone who counts on certain times of the month being "safe" times for having sex without birth control is taking a pretty big pregnancy risk.

A missed menstrual period is usually the first sign that a girl is pregnant.

A female becomes pregnant if a male's sperm unites with one of her eggs and the fertilized egg attaches in her uterus. A missed menstrual period is usually the first sign of pregnancy. Other signs of pregnancy include tender, swollen breasts, the need to urinate (pee) a lot, upset stomach (nausea or vomiting) especially in the morning and feeling very tired all the time. Clothing may also feel tighter.

If you think you may be pregnant, the only sure way to know is to have a pregnancy test. You can get a urine or blood test at your health care provider, a hospital or a clinic. (You can also test yourself with a home test kit purchased at the drugstore; follow the directions carefully.) Through a pelvic exam, a health care provider can see whether you are pregnant and how far along you are.

breaking the news

If you find that you or your partner is pregnant and you didn't plan it, you may find it hard to break the news to the people who are important in your life. But you could find it helpful to involve them in your decision about what to do.

Many teens are afraid that their parents will be angry. They worry that their parents will force them to choose an option they don't want.

The first reaction of most parents will be shock, which might be expressed as anger or sadness. They might yell or cry. But give them a chance to get over the shock. Later they'll probably be able to discuss your options in a helpful way.

If you don't feel that you can tell your parents, tell another trusted adult. An unplanned pregnancy is not the kind of problem for teens to handle on their own.

Breaking the news can be easier if you prepare. Think about what you'll say. Imagine the responses you might get and write them below the cartoons on this page. The first excercise is for girls only, the second is for both boys and girls.

Telling boyfriend

Telling parents

The thing I am afraid to hear

_____

What I think I'll hear

_____

What I hope to hear

_____

The thing I am afraid to hear

_____

What I think I'll hear

_____

What I hope to hear

_____

options in pregnancy

Lots of girls have experienced unintended pregnancy. If this happens to you, you will face two of the biggest decisions you'll ever make in your life — whether to continue the pregnancy, and whether to keep the baby if you do.

Note: If you think you might continue the pregnancy, see a health care provider to start prenatal (PREE-nay-tal) health care immediately. Prenatal means "before birth." Prenatal care can detect and correct most health problems that could harm the baby or mother. Babies who don't get this care are five times more likely to die than infants who do. And pregnancy makes a teen more likely to have serious medical problems.

Your decision about your pregnancy will have a big effect on your life, so think about it carefully. Ask yourself, your boyfriend and your parents some really hard questions. Here are some to ask:

- *Keeping the baby.* Are you ready for the lifetime responsibilities of being a parent? Does your partner share your feelings? How will the two of you support the baby?

- *Adoption.* How will you feel about giving birth and then giving up your baby? Do you think your baby will be better off with someone else? Can you handle a decision that is final?

- *Foster care.* How will you feel about being separated from your child? If your baby is placed with another family, what will you do to develop a relationship with him/her?

- *Abortion.* This is a medical procedure to end a pregnancy. It involves either surgery or the taking of pills containing mifepristone (pronounced miff-eh-priss-tone, also known as RU-486). Think back to your feelings about abortion before you became pregnant. Have your feelings changed? How do you think you will feel after the abortion? What are your family's feelings?

Decide carefully. Your decision will have a big effect on your life.

Whichever decision you make, you may sometimes regret it. Those feelings are normal and usually pass with time. But if you can't stop being upset about your decision, counseling can help.

sexually transmitted diseases

Symptoms

Here are some symptoms that can warn of an STD, although sometimes there are no symptoms at all. If you are sexually active and experience any of these symptoms, see a health care provider immediately. If you notice any of these symptoms in a partner, don't have sex with that person.

- Sores, bumps or blisters near the sex organs, rectum or mouth.

- Unusual discharge or smell from the vagina. Clear or white "drip" from the penis. Any anal discharge.

- Burning or pain when urinating (peeing), or frequent urination.

- Sore or swollen throat after oral sex.

- Itching around the genitals.

- Rash, especially on the soles of the feet or the palms of the hands.

- Warts (hard, wrinkled bumps) around the genitals.

- Pain in your lower abdomen or swelling or pain in the area around your sex organs.

- Flu-like feelings with fever, chills and aches.

Itching and burning in the vaginal area can be caused by a yeast (YEEST) infection, which is *not* an STD and usually goes away with proper treatment. The same symptoms can also mean the STD trichomoniasis (trick-oh-moh-NEYE-ahh-sis) or "trick." Either way, you need to see your health care provider.

Diseases

These are the most common STDs, the way to pronounce each one, and the slang terms (if any) people may use when speaking of them:

- chlamydia (klem-ID-ee-ah), "burning"

- genital herpes (JEN-it-all HER-peez)

- gonorrhea (gawn-or-EE-ah), "the drip"

- hepatitis B* (heh-pah-TIE-tiss)

- HIV, or Human Immunodeficiency (im-MUNE-oh-dee-FISH-en-see) Virus, causes AIDS

- HPV*, or Human Papillomavirus (PAP-ill-oh-mah-VI-russ), causes genital (JEN-it-all) warts, and can cause cervical cancer

- syphilis (SIFF-ill-iss), "the clap"

The following are also transmitted by sexual activity, although they are not diseases:

- pubic lice, or "crabs," is a parasite (small insect pest)

- vaginitis (VAJ-a-NYE-tis) is an infection of the vagina

Note: Some people mistakenly believe that if they've already had an STD, they can't get it again. The truth is, getting an STD does not give you any immunity against getting it or some other STD again.

* These are the only STDs that can be prevented with a vaccination. Ask your health care provider.

STDs

People can get sick from many kinds of germs. Some sicknesses are passed from person to person by sexual contact. These illnesses are best known as sexually transmitted diseases, or STDs; although some people call them venereal diseases, or VD.

HIV is one of the STDs that you hear a lot about — we'll discuss it in on page 81. Here, our focus is the other STDs.

There are more than 25 STDs. Untreated, STDs will make you miserable with rashes, sores, itching, dripping and more (see page 78). Some can lead to serious health complications; for example, HPV can cause cervical cancer. Some can kill you. And if you're pregnant, some STDs can harm or kill your unborn baby.

These diseases pass from person to person during sex.

While STDs can be very dangerous, most can be cured — if treated early. Go to a clinic or a health care provider right away if you see any of the warning signs (page 78) on your body or your partner's. STDs will not go away without treatment; the symptoms may come and go, but the disease is there until treated.

As with most diseases, the best "cure" is prevention. It's very unlikely that you'll catch one of these diseases unless you have sex with a person who has it. If you are in a relationship and you decide to have sex, you and your partner can protect each other

from STDs by getting a health checkup first. It's unlikely that you'll catch an STD if you're having sex with only one healthy partner, and that partner only with you. If either you or your partner is also having sex with others, always use a condom.

Some STDs don't have symptoms that you can see, or the symptoms may not show up right away. If you decide to have sex without knowing whether your partner is healthy, you can get some protection from STDs by using a condom. Contraceptive creams and foams used with a diaphragm also offer some protection. (To review these birth control methods, see page 70.)

The national STD/AIDS hotline is 1-800-CDC-INFO or 1-800-232-4636. For emergency help in the Philadelphia area, call the CHOICE hotline at 215-985-3300. You can learn more about STDs by visiting the website of the American Social Health Association, www.ashastd.org, or the website of the Family Planning Council, www.familyplanning.org.

HIV + AIDS — myth vs. fact

How you get HIV:

• unprotected vaginal, oral or anal sex

• sharing needles

• breast feeding from an HIV-positive mother

You *can't* get HIV from:

• swimming in a pool with an infected person

• using public toilets

• living with, working with or talking with an infected person

• being friends with an HIV-positive person.

Although experts know you can't get HIV from sharing food or drinks with an infected person, it's still a good idea to avoid that. Lots of other germs are exchanged that way; Hepatitis, Mononucleosis and Meningitis are examples.

It's also wise to be careful about kissing an infected person. Although a casual kiss on the lips is safe, passionate French kissing can be risky. If the infected person's mouth has a tiny cut or sore, the virus can pass from his or her blood into your saliva and be carried into your blood.

Symptoms of AIDS:

• extreme tiredness for no reason

• rapid weight loss without dieting (more than 10 pounds in 2 months)

• stubborn dry cough

• frequent fever

• sweating while sleeping

• purple skin blotches, rashes, bumps or tumors

• skin bruises easily

• swollen glands in the neck, armpits and groin

• white coating on the tongue or throat

• trouble recovering from common minor illnesses

• recurrent vaginal yeast infections that do not respond to treatment

Note: None of these symptoms is a sure sign of AIDS. In fact, if you have not had unprotected sexual intercourse or shared a drug needle, it is almost certain that your symptoms are caused by something else. If you have any of the above health problems, see a health care provider. And if you think you might have been exposed to HIV, see a health care provider even if you have no symptoms at all.

Note: There are now medications that can be taken within 72 hours (3 days) of known exposure to HIV that can significantly decrease your chance of getting infected.

HIV + AIDS

HIV or Human Immunodeficiency (im-MUNE-oh-dee-FISH-en-see) Virus, is the virus that causes AIDS. The most common way to get HIV is by having unprotected sex — vaginal sex, anal sex or oral sex — with an infected person. HIV lives in body fluids such as blood, vaginal secretions and semen. The virus destroys the body's ability to fight diseases and infections. AIDS, which stands for Acquired Immune Deficiency Syndrome, is actually a series of diseases that take advantage of the weakened immune system in an HIV-positive person.

A lot of research is going on to find a cure for AIDS, and treatments are extending lives, but right now AIDS is deadly. Meanwhile, HIV-positive people — who may not know they are infected — are passing the virus to others. HIV is contagious long before the person who has it shows any symptoms. You can't tell by looking at a person whether he or she is HIV-positive.

A common way to get HIV is unprotected sex with an infected partner.

HIV was first thought to be spread through male homosexual activity, but now it is clear that anyone who is sexually active is at risk. More than 90 percent of all adolescent and adult HIV infections have resulted from heterosexual intercourse. Less common ways people get HIV are drug addicts sharing needles and mothers passing HIV to their babies.

If you are having sex, you can reduce your chances of infection by using a condom every time. You should always ask about your partner's past sexual activity. A person who's had sex with many people has had many chances to become infected. You can get HIV the first time you have sex.

If you think you might have been exposed to HIV, you need to go to a health care provider or a clinic for a test as soon as possible. A home HIV test kit also is available; follow the directions carefully. New treatments are helping HIV-positive people live longer and healthier lives. And the sooner you begin treatment, the more likely you will get its full benefit.

Always remember to protect yourself and the people you care about: Use a condom every time you have sex.

The national STD/AIDS hotline is 1-800-CDC-INFO or 1-800-232-4636. For emergency help in the Philadelphia area, call the CHOICE hotline at 215-985-3300. You can learn more about HIV/AIDS at www.familyplanning.org.

chapter 5

me + my safety

getting "high"

alcohol

cigarettes + tobacco

who's abused

disaster planning

Internet safety

posting pictures

online communities

violence

suicide

harmful drugs

People who misuse the drugs listed here find it hard to stop. Depending on the drug, they may be psychologically dependent (feeling strongly that they need it) or physically dependent (their body is addicted and they will feel very sick if they stop), or both.

Note: If you need immediate help with a drug problem, call the hotline operated by the National Alcohol and Substance Abuse Information Center: 1-800-784-6776.

Marijuana (mah-rih-WHON-ah)
slang: pot, grass, weed
The most commonly used illegal drug in the U.S., it's usually smoked in homemade cigarettes (joints or blunts), pipes or bongs. Can interfere with memory, making "stoned" users poor students; also reduces coordination, affecting driving skills. Long-term smokers damage their lungs. Hashish is concentrated marijuana usually smoked in pipes.

Cocaine (co-CANE); slang: coke, blow
Users inhale (snort) or inject this white powder. They get a strong high and an "I-can-do-anything" feeling, then they "crash." Can cause hallucinations (seeing things) and deadly seizures, especially when taken with alcohol or heroin. Addictive. In a very dangerous form known as crack, cocaine is smoked.

Ecstasy (EX-tah-see); slang: E, X
Users take this psychedelic drug in tablet or capsule form and experience a false sense of happiness and closeness with others. May cause permanent brain damage. Use has been linked to death caused by severe dehydration and overheating. "Liquid X" is a slang term for the very dangerous drug GHB (gamma hydroxybutyrate), which can cause coma or death.

Amphetamines (am-FET-ah-meens)
slang: speed, uppers, crystal meth
These drugs rev-up the nervous system and make the user feel full of energy. Severe side effects include heart problems and dependence. Overdoses can kill. Crystal methamphetamine also can produce psychotic symptoms such as violent behavior and paranoia that may persist for months or years. Users may get "meth mouth" — tooth loss and severe tooth decay.

Barbiturates (bar-BIT-chur-ats)
slang: downers
These and other sedatives slow down the nervous system to calm a person or cause sleep. Can cause addiction. Overdoses can kill. One type, Quaaludes, can cause horrible hallucinations. Some users die when they combine barbiturates with other drugs.

Heroin (HAIR-oh-win)
slang: dope, junk, scag, horse, smack, H
A narcotic that users inject, smoke or inhale (snort). Addiction is quick and very hard to kick. Addicts often overdose and die. Some get HIV from sharing needles.

Phencyclidine (fen-SIGH-clid-een)
slang: PCP, angel dust
Swallowed in capsules, smoked or injected, PCP affects the brain and can drive users to hurt or kill other people or themselves.

Note: No list of harmful drugs stays up-to-date for long because kids are always finding new ways to get high. Keep in mind that all illegal drugs are harmful — that's why they're illegal!

getting "high"

You may have heard the saying, "What goes up must come down." It's the law of gravity. It's also an important fact about drug use. People use drugs to "get high," but that "up" feeling doesn't last. In minutes or hours, the user "comes down." So he or she seeks another high. A cycle has begun.

When a person becomes dependent on a drug, the cycle of highs and lows becomes more dangerous, and more desperate. The person craves the drug so strongly that he or she may lie, cheat, steal or hurt others to get it. Meanwhile, the drug is causing serious harm to the user.

The cycle of highs and lows gets more and more desperate.

You probably know that illegal drugs such as Marijuana, Cocaine, Ecstasy, PCP and Heroin are harmful. You may not know that legal substances — prescription medicine or ordinary household products, for example — can also be harmful if used in the wrong way. (See also page 87 on alcohol and page 89 on cigarettes and tobacco.)

Some people misuse products such as cleaning solvents, glues and aerosols by breathing in their fumes to get high. "Huffing" replaces the oxygen your body needs with toxic gases that can damage vital organs, even kill you instantly.

Some people misuse drugs a health care provider has prescribed for them or for someone else. Drugs like Ritalin, Xanax and Percocet are legal "by prescription only" for a reason: Taken by the wrong person or in the wrong amount, they can be very dangerous.

Some people take illegal drugs not to get high but as a "short cut" to accomplish a goal, such as losing weight with amphetamines or getting bigger muscles with steroids. No goal is more important than staying healthy!

People you know and people you don't may urge you to try drugs. You may see users who appear to be very relaxed or very happy when they're high and you might think it would be nice to feel that way for awhile. But be smart and walk away. A temporary high is not worth damaging your health or your life.

Note: For help with a drug problem, check the yellow page listings under "Drug Abuse & Addiction." For more about huffing, go to www.inhalants.org.

booze and you

Role-playing — imagining yourself in a situation and maybe acting it out — is a great way to prepare for difficult situations. What would you do if:

• You were supposed to get a ride in a friend's car but the driver is drunk or high.

_____

_____

• One of your friends has gotten drunk at a party and is embarrassing you by acting really stupid.

_____

_____

• Your boyfriend or girlfriend wanted to apologize for insulting you when he/she was drunk last weekend.

_____

_____

• Someone you love has been drinking a lot lately and you think the person may be an alcoholic.

_____

_____

• You suspect your younger brother or sister is sneaking alcohol out of your parents' cupboard.

_____

_____

alcohol

Alcohol is a drug. Because it's a legal drug for adults, some teens see nothing wrong with using it even before they reach the legal drinking age.

Actually, there are many good reasons for teens to stay away from booze, now and in the future. Here are three for now:

• Like a poison, alcohol affects people with 100-pound bodies much more strongly than it affects people who weigh 180. It's easy for teens to drink too much without drinking much at all.

• It is not always easy to drink only in moderation and only in safe situations. Teens are learning how to act in new social situations, and adding alcohol makes it all the harder.

• Teens are learning to think about possible consequences before they act. Alcohol can make you act without thinking. It lowers your inhibitions, making you more likely to do or say stupid (and perhaps dangerous) things.

Teens wonder why drinking is okay for adults but not for them.

Even in the future when you reach the legal drinking age, you might well stay away from alcohol for other reasons. Teens who have seen others get drunk know that:

• drunk people often make fools of themselves in front of others,

• drunk people can be really nasty and abusive,

• drunk people sometimes throw up or pass out,

• drunk people can hurt the people they care about and love.

Some teens become binge drinkers. They drink massive amounts at one time. By binging — even on wine or beer — they run the risk of overdosing on alcohol. They could go into a coma or even die.

People can become addicted to alcohol. A person who cannot control the urge to drink is an alcoholic. If that person is you, or someone in your family, seek help from a group such as Alcoholics Anonymous (AA). A local chapter is listed in your phone book.

alien encounter

Imagine what visitors from another planet might think if they spent a week watching Earthlings smoke. What bewildering, strange and disgusting sights might they see? What might they conclude about why smokers smoke? Create a short dialogue between two alien visitors to dramatize what they see.

Alien One _____

_____

Alien Two _____

_____

Alien One _____

_____

Alien Two _____

cigarettes + tobacco

Have you ever watched an old cigarette smoker coughing and gagging at the beginning of a new day? The next time you do, think of this: Chances are, he or she started smoking at your age.

Once you start smoking, it's very hard to stop. That's because cigarettes contain the drug nicotine (NIK-oh-teen), which is addictive. Give your body a taste of nicotine and it will crave more.

Most smokers didn't intend to start an unhealthy habit. In fact, most of them didn't even enjoy their first cigarettes — they tasted bad, smelled worse, burned their throat and made them cough. They may have continued smoking because their friends were doing it, or because smoking fit in with an image they were trying to achieve, or because they thought smoking would help them lose weight (it doesn't). Later, they may have tried to quit and couldn't.

You don't have to wait decades to feel the effects of smoking.

Everyone knows smoking is a health hazard that can cause lung cancer, emphysema (em-fih-ZEE-mah), heart disease and other illnesses. Even non-smokers can develop health problems from breathing smokey air ("second-hand smoke"). At your age, those health problems may seem too far away to matter. But you don't have to wait decades to experience the effects of smoking. Teen smokers may find they cough a lot, get sicker from colds, watch their white teeth turn yellow and their breath turn stale, see tiny wrinkles on their skin, and feel short of breath when playing a sport.

If you don't smoke, don't start. Why cause yourself health problems you can easily avoid? To protect yourself from the dangers of "second-hand" smoke, politely ask others not to smoke around you. If they refuse, move away.

Notes: Cigars, cigarillos, chewing tobacco and snuff also have enough nicotine to get you hooked. They, too, can cause cancer. Don't be fooled that cigarettes advertised as "natural" are healthy. They're not. They still contain tobacco —and nicotine. And finally, the government recently banned most flavored cigarettes because the flavorings make them taste sweeter but do nothing to reduce the damage they will cause to your body. If you crave chocolate or vanilla, buy an ice cream cone instead!

89

st⚉pping abuse

Many young people who are abused don't tell anyone, so they don't get the help they need to stop the abuse. Here are three reasons they don't tell. For each one, answer the question that follows.

1. A big reason victims don't tell is that they know the abuser, usually quite well. It's much harder to point a finger at someone you have feelings for, such as a boyfriend, a relative or a youth group leader.

- If a friend told you he/she was being abused, what could you say to convince your friend to tell a trusted adult — even though it would be hard?

2. Some victims don't tell because they think the hurt they suffer is punishment for being "bad," even if they didn't do anything wrong. They may believe they are guilty of something because they "make" the abuser hurt them. They may feel that if they just try harder to please the abuser, the abuse will stop.

- If your friend told you about things that happened that clearly sounded abusive to you, what could you say to convince your friend that it *was* abuse, it was wrong, and he/she should tell a trusted adult?

3. Some victims don't tell because they're too scared. They may be afraid no one will believe them, afraid the abuse will get worse if the abuser finds out they told, or afraid of what will happen to the family if an abusive family member is sent to jail.

- If your friend told you he/she was being abused but was too scared to tell, what could you say to help your friend overcome those fears and tell a trusted adult?

If you are being abused and feel you can't tell any adult you know, or you've told already but no one you know will help you, don't give up. You can get help by calling one of the local numbers listed under "abuse" in the blue pages of the telephone book. You also can call the National Child Abuse Hotline. It's a free call and you don't have to give your name. You can talk freely and get advice about what to do or whom to call in your area. Trained people answer this hotline 24 hours a day:

National Child Abuse Hotline
1-800-4-A-CHILD or 1-800-422-4453

who's abused

Sometimes people use their power to control others in ways that harm them physically, sexually or emotionally. We call this abuse. Abuse suffered when a person is young can cause problems that last far into the future, including depression, nightmares and difficulty forming close relationships. Abuse is *never* the victim's fault. Here are some examples of abuse.

Physical abuse: You have been abused if another person has hurt you by pushing you, kicking you, choking you, hitting you or punching you.

Sexual abuse: You have been abused if another person has forced you to touch their sex organs or has touched yours without your permission. This is often called molesting. If another person forces you to have sexual intercourse, you are not only abused, you are a victim of rape. Rape is a crime. Children and young teens are considered victims of "statutory rape" if they have sexual intercourse with an older teen or adult, whether or not they were forced to. A very damaging form of sexual abuse is incest: when a family member has sexual contact with a young relative.

Emotional abuse: You have been abused if another person often threatens to hurt or severely punish you, constantly insults you and puts you down, or keeps you from talking to or seeing other people for long periods of time.

> Abusive people use their power to control others who are less powerful.

In every abusive situation, the abuser is more powerful than the person being abused. The power may be physical — an abuser who is bigger and stronger. The power may be psychological — an abuser who is an authority figure, such as a parent, teacher or coach, older sister/brother or other relative. Abusers sometimes try to scare people by making threats. Others try to control people by buying them expensive gifts, alcohol or drugs.

Young teens are vulnerable to abuse because they lack power, but they do have the power to ask for help. If you or a friend of yours is a victim of physical, sexual or emotional abuse, tell a trusted adult. Don't wait. Tell now. And if the first adult you tell doesn't believe you, tell someone else. Keep telling until someone helps you.

91

be prepared

The American Red Cross publishes these guidelines for disaster planning. Share the information on this page with an adult in your family.

1. Create a Family Disaster Plan

- Contact your local Red Cross chapter and your local emergency management or civil defense office to learn which disasters are most likely to happen in your community.

- Meet with your family to discuss the types of disasters that could occur and how you will respond.

- Discuss what to do if you are advised to evacuate.

- Plan how your family will stay in contact if separated by disaster. Identify two meeting places:
  1) a location a safe distance from your home in case you can't get back into your house
  2) a place outside your neighborhood in case you can't return to the neighborhood right away.

- Choose an out-of-state friend as a "check-in contact" for everyone to call. Make sure each family member knows the contact's phone number.

- Create a Disaster Supply Kit complete with food, water and clothing. (Contact your local Red cross chapter for a complete list of supplies.)

2. Complete this Checklist

_ Post emergency telephone numbers by every phone.

_ Teach responsible family members how and when to shut off water, gas and electricity at main switches.

_ Install a smoke detector on each level of your home, especially near bedrooms; test monthly and change the batteries twice each year.

_ Contact your local fire department to learn about home fire hazards.

_ Learn First Aid and CPR through your local American Red Cross chapter.

3. Practice and Maintain Your Plan

- Conduct fire and emergency evacuation drills.

- Quiz each other every six months so everyone remembers what to do.

- Maintain and replace old items in your Disaster Supply Kit.

- Contact your local Red Cross chapter and ask for a copy of "Your Family Disaster Plan" and the " Emergency Preparedness Checklist."

disaster planning

When there's a disaster in the world, you hear about it. News travels almost instantly around the globe; first by television, radio, and the Internet; then by word of mouth from person to person to you. There's no escaping news about the latest earthquake, hurricane, flood, blizzard, tornado or volcanic eruption. And sadly, war and terrorism make news just as often. It can seem as though something horrible is happening every day.

When you're seeing reports of a disaster, it's natural to feel sorry for the people who are suffering and want to help them. It's also natural to be glad that, this time, you're not one of them. And it's perfectly natural to wonder whether an equally awful disaster could someday happen to you or people you love.

Having a plan will make you feel more safe and secure.

If you do wonder about that, it probably makes you feel a little fearful, anxious or uneasy. Most young people get over those feelings fairly quickly as the news fades from the headlines and they re-focus on school, friends and activities. If you find you just can't shake your anxiety and it is interfering with enjoyment of your daily life, talk about it with a parent, clergy or school counselor.

While merely worrying about a future disaster that might never happen gets you nowhere, making an emergency plan with your family is a really good idea. You will feel more safe and secure just knowing that there is a plan to follow if something unexpected happens.

Parents and teens want the same thing in an emergency: to be in contact immediately and be together as soon as possible. So most emergency plans start with how family members will contact one another. In some families everyone carries a cell phone with family members on speed dial. For them, the first step in an emergency is a cell phone call. If that doesn't work, a second step might be for everyone to call the same out-of-town relative, or for everyone to meet at a pre-selected place.

If you don't already know your family's emergency plan, ask about it. If your family doesn't have one, you can suggest a family meeting to discuss it.

do & don't online

As you explore the Internet, remember these DOs and DON'Ts.

DO discuss your favorite Web sites with your parents.

DON'T give out personal information such as your real name, address, phone number, where you go to school, parents' names, credit card number or password — even if it is requested for a contest entry.

DO report any threat of violence to a trusted adult. You could prevent someone from getting hurt.

DON'T ever post or forward anything you know to be untrue.

DO alert your Internet Service Provider (such as Comcast or Verizon) of any site that shows violence or pornography, uses offensive language or promotes illegal activity.

DON'T agree to meet anyone in person without a parent's permission.

DO discuss anything that bothers or troubles you online with a trusted adult.

DON'T create any Web site designed to put down, slander or threaten teachers, schools or other kids. Everything on the Internet can be traced, and anyone you put down will hear about it eventually.

DO respect any limits your parents set on the sites you can visit online.

DON'T think there is such a thing as complete privacy online. With today's technology and the ability of "hackers" you're better off believing that anything you write can be accessed by someone.

Internet safety

The Internet is a great way to keep in touch with your friends. Getting e-mail and sending instant messages is a lot of fun. You can also use the Net to do research for a homework assignment, follow your favorite sports teams, check out the latest songs and see what's going to be showing at the movie theater.

While the Internet is giving us new ways to communicate, get information and be entertained, it is also posing new dangers to young people. Some people using the Net, social networking sites, chats and instant messaging (IMing) are looking for ways to use you or even harm you. So you have to be careful.

Beware of anyone who asks you for personal information like where you live, your full name, where you go to school, your parents' names, a credit card number, your password or your phone number. Don't tell them — even if they claim to be working for an Internet Service Provider, such as Comcast or Verizon, or a social networking site, like Facebook. Keep your password a secret. Don't even tell your best friend.

Be careful to avoid the creeps online as you do in "the real world."

Often the people who are asking for personal information just want to send you and your family annoying advertisements. But some of them are trying to steal from you. And some of them want to meet you so that they can use you or hurt you. This is pretty rare, but it does happen.

The fact that there are some creeps online shouldn't freak you out. There are creeps in "the real world" too and you've learned how to avoid them, right? You just have to be more careful about avoiding creeps online because there they can pretend to be someone else, get your attention and win your trust. If an IM, a texting conversation or an e-mail message makes you feel uncomfortable or scared, write down the sender's screen name, sign off and tell a trusted adult right away.

If you feel that you've made a new friend online, it's natural to want to meet that person, but it can be dangerous. Talk it over with a trusted adult. Some adults might say yes to a meeting if they go with you and the meeting is in a public place.

before you post

Before you post or forward a picture, take a minute and ask yourself these questions:

1. Am I making a smart decision right now? Or am I sending this picture because I am feeling angry, anxious or out of control?

2. Will I feel differently about this picture tomorrow? Next week? A year from now? Ten years from now?

3. Would other people I respect and care about feel differently about me if they knew I took this picture, posed for it, posted it or forwarded it?

4. By sharing this photo, do I risk hurting a friendship or another relationship that's important to me?

5. Could I or anyone else in the picture get in trouble if the picture is seen by a parent, a school principal or a police officer?

posting pictures

Many people use cell phones, cameras and websites like Facebook to express themselves and keep up to date with their friends. You can show a friend the shoes you're planning to wear to the dance — just take a picture and send it. You can impress the world with your dog's new trick — just record a video and upload it.

Pictures and videos like that are harmless and fun. But you can harm yourself and others — and get in lots of trouble — by sending or posting photos and videos that could be embarrassing or illegal.

It's something to think about *before* you post or e-mail anything on the Internet or send it to a cell phone. After you hit "send" it will be too late: You have lost control over those images.

Post a picture on a website and anyone can copy it, download it, forward it or post it on another site. If you regret the posting later, it's already too late. You may never find all the copies. They could still be "out there" many years from now.

If you regret the posting later, it's already too late.

Even a picture you send to a friend's cell phone is not completely safe. The friend probably won't forward it (unless you break up or she gets mad at you...) but that phone could be borrowed or stolen.

Before you post or send a photo, ask yourself whether it's okay for everyone to see it. Everyone includes: your parents, your teachers, your brothers and sisters, people you don't like, people you have crushes on, and your minister or clergy person.

With this in mind:

• Never post or send naked pictures of yourself. Aside from potential embarrassment, naked pictures could get you in legal trouble for creating pornography.

• Never ask anybody for naked pictures or forward any that are sent to you. You risk damaging important relationships and could get into legal trouble for distributing pornography.

• Never post or send pictures of yourself or your friends drinking alcohol or doing anything else that's illegal. See "embarrassment" and "legal trouble" above.

97

good site, bad site

People can get lots of bad information on the Internet, leading them to believe things that aren't true and to trust people who aren't trustworthy.

When you're on the Internet, you need to use your critical thinking skills and look for clues that tell you if the site can be trusted.

If you ask yourself these questions, you'll get plenty of clues to help you decide whether you've found a good site or a bad site.

1. **Am I keeping my visits to the site a secret?**
   If you haven't mentioned the site to any of your friends or family members, that's a big clue it's a bad site. Keeping it a secret is a sign that you are ashamed or embarrassed by what you're reading and seeing on the site. You already know it's bad. You just have to admit it to yourself and decide to spend your online time elsewhere.

2. **Do I know who is supplying the information?**
   Every website should have information about the person or group responsible for the site, and a way to contact them by mail, phone or email. If those things are lacking, the site owner is hiding — a big clue that it's a site to avoid. If the site owner is well known and has a great reputation, that's a big clue that the site is reliable.

3. **Can I verify the information elsewhere?**
   It's extremely rare that truthful information is found in only one place. You can quickly test a suspicious statement by checking other sites you already know you can trust. For example, if you read something on a health topic and wonder if it's true, you can go to a national site like WebMD or the site of a hospital in your area to see what they say on the same topic.

Note: It's normal to talk with friends and family about the websites you are visiting, just as you talk about the music you are listening to and the TV shows you are watching. It's a great way to have some interesting conversations, to learn about other sites you might like, and to test the way people you care about react to the sites you tell them about.

online communities

If you like a certain game, band, team, hobby, activity or TV show, there's a good chance it has websites, blogs and Internet communities dedicated to it. They're a good place to learn more about your favorite stuff and to see what other people have to say about it.

But some online communities and social groups promote unhealthy or hateful ideas and behaviors. These groups tend to be small and members keep their true identities hidden because they know the ideas and behaviors they promote are not accepted in our society. Yet the fact they have a website can make them seem okay.

For example, there are "Pro Ana" websites that promote anorexia, which is an unhealthy and sometimes fatal eating disorder (see page 17). These sites tell young people that being underweight is attractive and it's good to starve themselves.

Hate groups have websites, too. These sites uses lies and half-truths to tell visitors why they should hate people of different races, countries or religions, or people who are gay or lesbian.

Join online groups that share your interests and values.

Free speech laws protect these sites unless they encourage illegal, violent or terrorist activities. So the best thing to do is ignore them. But if you have a friend who is visiting sites like these, encourage your friend to talk about it with a trusted adult. Or give your friend the "Good Site, Bad Site" guide on page 98.

While there are bad communities doing negative things on the Web, there are far more good communities doing positive things. Through websites and social networks like Facebook, you can join efforts to fight animal cruelty, stop global warming or save the rainforests. You can help raise money for charities that are trying to find cures for diseases or help people in poverty. You can become a "fan" of a politician, a celebrity or a group that is helping make the world a better place. You can even start a "cause" of your own and tell all the people in your network why they should support it.

Steer clear of online communities that promote unhealthy or hateful ideas and behaviors. Spend your time in the ones that connect you with people who share your interests and values.

dealing with anger

Anger is a strong emotion. It's hard not to feel angry sometimes, but you can control how you act on your feelings. Stop and think for a minute about the ways you deal with anger.

Things that make me angry
List three things that have made you angry recently, such as, "When my parents didn't let me go to a party."

1.

2.

3.

How I know I am angry
List three things that happen to you when you feel angry, such as, "My heart starts to beat faster."

1.

2.

3.

How I can deal with my anger
List three things you have done, or could do, to handle your angry feelings, such as, "Call a friend and talk about it."

1.

2.

3.

Are any of the ways you deal with anger violent? If so, you need to talk with a trusted adult about finding non-violent ways to handle your anger. Violence never solves anything.

vi**o**lence

Everyone gets angry about stuff sometimes. It's okay. But sometimes anger turns into violence, which is definitely *not okay*. Sudden violent acts — like school shootings — may seem to "come out of nowhere" but in reality they come from anger.

One teen might be feeling angry because he's being teased or picked on at school. He might think hurting others will get him the respect he deserves. A violent act probably would make him feared — but the respect he really wants comes from positive action, not aggression.

Another teen might feel angry because she's lonely and needs attention. She might "act out" by making threats. What she really wants is to make friends or make her friendships stronger, and sadly her actions are just pushing people away.

People who are about to become violent often give warnings.

A third teen might be throwing punches in an angry reaction to abuse he is suffering or seeing at home.

You may be able to de-fuse another teen's anger in some cases by telling the teasers to stop, including a person who's often left out, or being a sympathetic listener to someone who's upset. It's worth a try.

How do you know when a person is so angry that he or she may become violent? Often there are warning signs. By taking these warnings seriously, you can help keep your school and community safe. Tell a trusted adult if you know someone who: loses their temper a lot, damages or destroys property, has detailed plans to commit acts of violence, increases use of drugs and alcohol, threatens to hurt others, carries a weapon, has a fascination with weapons or enjoys hurting animals.

If you recognize any of these warning signs in yourself, get help immediately from a social worker or counselor or another trusted adult.

If someone is threatening you, tell an adult in authority who can protect you. Trying to protect yourself by carrying a weapon, or by fighting back with more violence, only makes the problem worse.

suicide warning signs

A person who is in danger of committing suicide might...

- Be depressed
- Feel suddenly much better after a deep depression
- Talk of suicide or talk of death as a "way out"
- Admit to having attempted suicide before
- Have a plan for how they would kill themselves
- Have access to a way of killing themselves, such as pills or a gun
- Have a change in appetite (either can't seem to eat anything or eats much more)
- Change their sleep habits (sleeps more than usual or has trouble falling asleep)
- Show a dramatic change in school performance
- Neglect their appearance or hygiene
- Use drugs or alcohol more than usual

- Feel very guilty
- Feel very anxious
- Feel very hopeless
- Feel very helpless
- Have a lot of difficulty recovering from a loss, such as the breakup of an important relationship or the death of a loved one
- Make a will
- Give away prized possessions
- Run away from home
- No longer enjoy activities they used to like
- Cut off important relationships
- Withdraw from friends

If you have a friend who might be in danger of suicide, tell a trusted adult immediately, even if you promised not to tell. Saving your friend's life is more important than breaking a promise!

If you have thoughts of suicide, GET HELP. Tell a trusted adult or call a suicide prevention hotline, like 1-800-273-TALK (8255) or 1-800-SUICIDE (784-2433).

suicide

Sometimes when people find themselves feeling extremely upset, stressed, hurt, angry, scared, lonely, sad or embarrassed they think about killing themselves. In most cases they don't really want to die, they just want to stop hurting.

It can feel really, really bad when you break up with a girlfriend or boyfriend, disappoint your family, feel different or left out or lose a friend. It can seem like suicide is the only answer.

But suicide is never an answer, it's just a permanent end. *All* problems can be dealt with in some other way. Even if the problem can't be solved, the pain it is causing now will gradually fade with time.

Talking about your feelings with a friend, a therapist, a clergy member or any trusted adult can help.

If feelings of hopelessness don't go away after a few weeks, you might be depressed. Depression can be treated and you can feel better (see page 31).

If you're being abused — emotionally, physically or sexually (see page 91) — seek help from a trusted adult. You need to get out of that situation to feel better.

Killing yourself is never an answer, it is just an end.

Sometimes one person committing suicide in the community can lead to others also trying it in "copycat" fashion. Just because someone else decides to kill themselves, it doesn't make suicide a good solution to your problems.

Remember that there *are* people who will listen and will help you and will accept you for who you are.

If you are thinking about suicide, most cities and towns have a 24-hour suicide prevention hotline you can call. Or you can call a national hotline, like 1-800-273-TALK (8255) or 1-800-SUICIDE (784-2433).

Sometimes life can be really rough and painful, but keep in mind that it can also be a lot of fun. It just might take a little while to get back to the fun part.

chapter 6

me + my family

relating

communicating

house rules

money matters

privacy

family crisis

looking at your family

All families are unique.

When you spend time at your friends' homes, you probably notice that your friends' families are different from yours. Maybe they are louder, or more formal, or have different rules, or are sillier with each other, or are more religious.

Some kids aren't biologically related to their parents and siblings, and some are. Some kids look like their parents and some don't.

There's no such thing as a typical family.

And parents come in all shapes and sizes, including: one mom, one dad, grandparents, a mom and a dad, two moms, two dads, foster parents and step parents.

Think about what makes your family special.

What's your favorite thing to do with your family? _____

What's the funniest story you have about your family? _____

_____

What are your family's favorite foods? _____

What things are important to your family? _____

How does your family celebrate good news? _____

What's your favorite memory of a time spent with your family? _____

_____

What story gets told and retold in your family? _____

_____

_____

What's your favorite thing about your family? _____

_____

relating

Experts call puberty the "stormy years" for young people and their families. If you and the adults at home are having more arguments than you used to, you're not alone.

At your age, you're beginning to change from a child to an adult. You feel you're ready for more freedom; the adults who care for you feel you still need their guidance. You're both right. And you both know that the limits on your behavior will have to expand slowly as you mature.

During this phase of your life you may clash with your parents* over curfews, chores, your clothing, your hairstyle, your choice of friends.

The key to positive parent-child relations is respect: self-respect and mutual respect.

Parents can demonstrate respect for themselves and their role by refusing to let a child bully them, insult them, lie to them, manipulate them, or embarrass them. By showing self-respect and setting a good example, parents earn a child's respect.

You want more freedom, but you still need adult guidance.

You can demonstrate self-respect by making the most of your intelligence, talents and personal appearance. When you are trustworthy and trying hard to be the best *you* possible, you earn the respect of your parents.

When you respect each other, it's easier to see disagreements between people who love and care for each other as part of life. It allows you to focus on the problem itself rather than blaming the other person for "causing" the problem. Mutual respect motivates you to resolve the problem in a way that preserves everyone's self-respect.

*Reminder: Wherever you see the word "parents" we are talking about the adult person or persons who take care of you. We recognize that children are raised in many kinds of families.

listening skills

Communicating well involves talking: putting your thoughts and feelings into words so that others can understand you. But communicating well also involves active listening: encouraging other people to express their thoughts and feelings in a way that you can understand.

By becoming a better listener you become a better communicator. Here are some examples of good (G) and bad (B) listening behaviors. Check off the boxes to show which ones are which. (Answers at the bottom of this page.)

	G	B	Listening Behavior
1.	☐	☐	staring off into the distance
2.	☐	☐	looking speaker in the eye
3.	☐	☐	saying "uh-huh" or nodding as speaker makes a point
4.	☐	☐	taking a deep breath and holding it
5.	☐	☐	crossing your arms in front of your chest
6.	☐	☐	asking follow-up questions, such as "What did you mean when you said…"
7.	☐	☐	rolling your eyes
8.	☐	☐	sighing loudly
9.	☐	☐	interrupting
10.	☐	☐	briefly repeating the main point when the speaker is finished: "So, you want me to…"

Answers 1. bad, 2. good, 3. good, 4. bad, 5. bad, 6. good, 7. bad, 8. bad, 9. bad, 10. good

c⊚mmunicating

"I just can't talk to my parents!"

Every teen since the beginning of time has probably made that complaint at some point.

Here are some things you can do to communicate better with the adults in your family in problem situations:

- *The topic makes you and/or your parents uncomfortable.* Perhaps it is sex, dating, drugs, alcohol, smoking, or divorce. Try looking for answers together in a book or DVD on the subject. You'll be surprised how that shifts the focus from your relationship to the problem.

- *You can't get the attention of busy parents.* Ask them if you can make an appointment for a talk. If you can't get their attention long enough to ask, leave them a note.

The m⊚re you talk t⊚ them, the better they'll under- stand.

- *You don't know how to tell your parents that you're upset about something they did.* Instead of accusing or blaming, which will make them defensive, tell them how the thing they did affected you. Begin your sentences with "I feel."

- *Your parents make you feel as though your concerns are unimportant.* If they say things like "That's silly," or "Oh, don't worry about *that*," or "You think *you* have problems," you have a perfect right to say back: "I feel hurt when you don't take me seriously. I'm asking you to listen."

- *You think they don't understand you.* Hey, only *you* really understand you. Parents are not mind-readers; you have to tell them what's going on in your head and heart. You have to put your thoughts and feelings into words. The more you talk to them, the better they'll understand you. They *can* understand — they were your age once!

Note: If you're worried that you'll forget what you wanted to say once a discussion gets going, make some notes beforehand that you can use as reminders.

preparing to discuss rules

Let's say you want to ask your parents for a later curfew so that you can spend more time with your friends. Of course they will respond to *what* you want, but they will also respond to *how* you ask.

Asking in a good way doesn't guarantee you'll get what you want immediately. However, asking in a bad way almost guarantees you won't get it anytime soon.

Asking in a good way means several things. It means choosing a good time and place to ask, using a polite tone of voice, making a request instead of a demand, and accepting the response graciously.

Explore ways of asking by reading the following situations. Which one is most likely to help you get what you want, A or B? (Answers at the bottom of this page.)

1. Time and place

A. You ambush your parents as they are walking in the door after work.

B. You wait until your little brothers and sisters are asleep to ask your parents if they will please join you at the kitchen table for a conversation.

2. Tone of voice

A. You speak calmly and confidently.

B. You whine or shout your request.

3. Request vs. demand

A. You say, "Now that I'm older, I'd like to be allowed to stay out later sometimes."

B. You say, "I'm old enough to stay out later and you have to let me!"

4. If they say "no"

A. You say, "I knew you'd say that. You never let me do anything."

B. You propose a compromise such as, "Instead of a later curfew every weekend, would you consider letting me stay out later for a special occasion? Then, if that works out, maybe we could talk about other occasions."

house rules

Every society has laws that govern the way people behave in public. When the laws are obeyed, everyone in the society can enjoy safety and order. Most people do obey because they value safety and order.

Every family has rules that govern the way family members behave at home. The rules are based on what the family leaders think is right and wrong. Those values may go beyond safety and order to include such things as neatness, cleanliness, polite manners, modest dress, sharing household duties, or being on time.

Sometimes families, like societies, have to enforce their rules by punishing people who break them. In our society a lawbreaker might have to go to jail for awhile. In your family a child who breaks a rule might lose a privilege for awhile.

You may think the rules of your house are too strict. Many people your age feel that way. Now that you're ready for more responsibilities, rules can seem like annoying roadblocks.

It makes sense for some house rules to be discussed and updated as you mature. You can suggest the family have a regular update discussion, maybe around the time of your birthday.

You want a rule changed or dropped? First, obey it well.

If you're planning to ask for a loosening of some rule next year, make a point of obeying it well this year. For example, if you want permission to stay out later on weekend nights, be sure you are returning home on time now. That shows your parents that you are responsible and can be trusted.

If you slip up and violate a house rule, accept responsibility. The mature thing to do is to admit your mistake, apologize and discuss what steps you'll take to prevent it from happening again.

wishes, goals and plans

We make wishes when we blow out birthday candles or toss a penny into a fountain. A wish is not a goal. Let's explore the differences.

A wish is something you want, but have no specific plan to get. Often a wish is beyond your control, such as "I wish my legs were longer." List three wishes here (no fair wishing for more wishes!):

1. _____

2. _____

3. _____

A goal is something you want that is within your power to get — if you plan and work to get it. List three goals here:

1. _____

2. _____

3. _____

Below, write a plan to achieve one of the three goals you set.

_____

_____

_____

money matters

If you're like most people, you'd like to have a little more cash to buy sneakers or earrings, or whatever. What do you want from the money in your life?

To get what you really want from money, it's important to set goals and know how much they cost. A goal is not a wish. It is something that you want so much you will make a real effort to get it. It's a specific target at which you aim and shoot. Buying an electronic game is a short-term goal; buying a car when you get your license is a long-term goal.

When you set goals, here are some of the good things that happen:

• You don't waste money on things you don't really want.

• You can give up the things that are less important to get the things that are more important.

• You are happy even if you are working hard, because you look forward to the reward you know you will get.

Most long-term goals cost a lot of money. Sometimes, you must give up short-term goals to reach your long-term goals.

No one gets everything they want, but there is a way to get most of what you want. The way is to make a plan. A plan is a step-by-step, written account of the things you must do to reach your goal.

There is a way to get most of what you want.

Getting something you want by shoplifting, stealing, or selling drugs is not only illegal but stupid. Odds are that you will get caught, if not immediately then eventually. At that point you will have a permanent criminal record, making it very difficult for you to get a job when you are an adult. In the meantime, you will be living with guilt, fear and shame. No one wants that.

my dream retreat

Describe the place you retreat to when you want to be alone.
What do you see there when you look around?

_____

What things do you have there?

_____

What do you do there?

_____

Now describe your fantasy retreat, the most ideal retreat you can imagine.
What would you see there when you looked around?

_____

What things would you have there?

_____

What would you do there?

_____

Compare your real retreat and your dream retreat.
What could you do to make your real retreat more like your dream?

_____

_____

privacy

Everyone needs privacy; during puberty it's crucial. You need a place where you can retreat and be alone with your thoughts.

Is there a closed-door policy at your house? In many families, one house rule is that a closed door means knock before entering.

Sometimes younger brothers and sisters are the biggest problems when it comes to your privacy. They aren't old enough yet to understand why you might prefer to be alone instead of with them.

Maybe you share a bedroom with a brother or sister. You could talk to your parents about using partitions or re-arranging the furniture to create private spaces in the room for each of you. You and your brother or sister might work out an agreement about how to give each other the space you need. Each one could have certain times to be alone in the room.

Boys and girls need space, a place and time to be alone.

During puberty some teens become very modest about their naked bodies and do not want family members to see them without clothes on. You may want to ask your family to respect your privacy when you're dressing or bathing.

You also may need more emotional privacy. Even if you're not keeping your thoughts tucked away in a journal under lock and key, you may want to guard them in other ways. Your parents may ask you more questions than you'd like about what happened during your day or what you are thinking. Sometimes you won't feel like talking, and you may be annoyed at all the questions.

Try to understand that parents care about their children and worry if they have no information. When you don't communicate, they may imagine the worst sorts of problems. Keep those communication lines open on as many conversation topics as you can. If you don't want to talk about your day, for example, try showing interest in theirs. Or shift the conversation to a topic you're both interested in, such as sports or movies or something that's in the news that day.

who can help?

People I know who could help in a family crisis

List the adults you trust enough to call in a crisis, whether the crisis is in your family or the family of a friend. Look up their phone numbers and write them here.

Name	Relationship*	Phone number
_____	_____	_____
_____	_____	_____
_____	_____	_____
_____	_____	_____
_____	_____	_____

* The person's relationship to you might be a relative, a health care provider, a leader at your place of worship, or the parent of a friend. Are there teachers, guidance counselors or other adults at your school who might be helpful in a crisis? Even if you can't find their phone numbers, you can list their names because you see them often and can talk to them in person.

People trained to help families in crisis

Get your local phone book and turn to the blue pages with the headline HUMAN SERVICES. For each type of crisis, write down the name and number of at least one agency where you could find trained people to help.

Type of crisis	Name of agency	Phone number
Abuse or Assault	_____	_____
Alcohol & Drug Problems	_____	_____
Counseling (family & personal)	_____	_____
Food - Money - Clothing	_____	_____

family crisis

Young people can get caught up in family problems that they didn't cause and can't solve. Maybe your family is having problems. Families today are under a lot of pressure. Serious issues a family might face include divorce, money worries brought on by loss of a job, loss of welfare benefits or loss of health insurance; drugs, alcohol, illness and abuse.

It's hard to feel happy or do well in school when things are bad at home. Some teens feel so helpless to change the family situation that they run away from home, thinking they'll escape to a better life. In fact, the life of a runaway almost always gets worse.

If you have a friend who's going through a crisis at home, you can offer a lot of help by being a good listener. Even if you can't solve the problem, you're giving your friend the relief that comes with confiding in another person. Try to convince your friend to confide in a trusted adult as well. An adult may be allowed to help in a way you can't.

Divorce, job loss, illness: families are under a lot of pressure.

If you are unhappy at home because of a family crisis, talk about it with a trusted adult. The adult could be a relative, a teacher or guidance counselor at school, a health care provider, a leader at your church, or the parent of a friend.

Some kids are nervous about contacting a professional counselor about their problems. In fact, social workers, counselors, psychiatrists and psychologists who work with teens are very easy to talk to. They're trained to know just what to do when a kid comes to them.

You can look in the yellow pages of the telephone book under "Counselors" to find agencies that help children and families get help. Don't let worries about cost keep you from calling. Some places provide free or low-cost services.

The National Youth Crisis Hotline number is 1-800-442-HOPE (4673).

chapter 7

me + my school

popularity

groups + labels

making the grade

hallway harassment

popularity up close

List three kids you think are popular and answer the questions about each.

Name_____ ☐ stranger ☐ acquaintance ☐ good friend

List the top three qualities that make this person popular.
Circle Y (yes) or N (no) to show whether this is a quality you admire.

1. _____ Y N   2. _____ Y N   3. _____ Y N

If you don't like this person, what don't you like about him or her?

_____

Name_____ ☐ stranger ☐ acquaintance ☐ good friend

List the top three qualities that make this person popular.

1. _____ Y N   2. _____ Y N   3. _____ Y N

If you don't like this person, what don't you like about him or her?

_____

Name_____ ☐ stranger ☐ acquaintance ☐ good friend

List the top three qualities that make this person popular.

1. _____ Y N   2. _____ Y N   3. _____ Y N

If you don't like this person, what don't you like about him or her?

_____

Now think about yourself. Are the qualities you admire in popular people qualities you have, too? If not, are they qualities you could work to develop in yourself? Look at your reasons for *not* liking a popular person. You can't be the only one who sees this person's bad side. Could it be that popular people are imperfect, just as you are? That they are popular because they emphasize their best qualities? Think about it.

popularity

Are you popular? Unpopular? Somewhere in between?

Being popular means being well-liked by the people around you. Some people your age feel that being popular is very important. For others, popularity means nothing.

What makes a person popular? Most often, it's a friendly, outgoing personality. People generally like you if you speak and behave in ways that show you like *them*.

All of us are at least a little shy, a little afraid of being rejected if we approach someone new. When a friendly person approaches us, we're grateful. They made the effort; they took the risk. How could you *not* like someone who would do all that for you?

Sometimes it's easiest to start up a conversation with someone else when you are involved in the same activity. You might be sitting next to each other in band or participating in a walk to raise money for a cause or a charity. The interest you share gives you a topic. Ask the other person his or her opinion of something related to that topic. Ask an "essay" question, not one they can answer "yes" or "no."

If you can be friendlier, you can be more popular.

Okay, you can be friendlier, you say — but aren't popular people also good-looking and well-off? Well, some of them are. But people who are liked for the face they were born with or their parents' money are not always people to envy. They may worry that no one likes them for their true selves.

No matter how popular or unpopular a person is, everyone wants good friends who like them for their true selves. A popular person may hang out with a larger group and have more admirers than a person who isn't popular. But popular people don't necessarily have more good friends.

It takes time and effort to develop good friendships. A person who thinks he or she has to win a popularity contest by constantly making more and more so-called friends may not find the time or energy to develop the deeper friendships that really count.

which in-crowd?

A tight social group — a clique or a crowd — can create a lot of pressure on its members to conform. They may pick up speech patterns and fashions they see modeled by the group's unofficial leaders.

groups + labels

Think about your peers at school. If one classmate were named and you had to describe him or her, chances are you would do it with a label — "he's a jock," "she's a brain," etc.

Probably he hangs out with a group of kids you call "the jocks," and she hangs out with a group you call "the brains." A group label somehow gets attached to everyone in it.

Which social group would your classmates say you belong to? Now, think about how you fit — or don't fit — the label. Do you like being labeled? In fact, all labels are too simple. Every person is much too complicated to be defined by one quality or interest.

If he's "a jock" and she's "a brain," what are you?

The social groups at your school may be called "crowds" or "cliques" (pronounced: clicks). In some schools, kids pay a lot of attention to which clique they're in. At other schools, it's not so important.

Cliques have their good and bad points. It's nice to have the feeling of belonging that goes with being part of a social group. (Why do you think some wealthy people join country clubs? Even adults have their cliques.) Cliques can be a lot of fun and a good way for teens to have fun in groups without pairing off into the boy-girl thing.

But there are other things about tight social groups that aren't so great. Sometimes cliques make people who are on the outside feel like losers. They can also make it harder for people in the clique to get to know other people outside it. And cliques can create strong peer pressure to do or say what the group does. Group members may feel it's so important to blend in that they mimic the speech patterns and fashions of the group's unofficial leaders.

Whether you become part of a clique or you don't, it might help to know that your membership in a teen social group doesn't have a thing to do with the adult life you'll lead. Some of the most successful people in the world felt like outsiders during their teenage years.

learning styles

When it comes to learning, people have their own styles. There are things you are good at and things you are not so good at. Answer these questions, and you'll know more about making the most of your learning style.

If you're having trouble with school-work or homework, consider sharing your answers with your teacher and parents. Knowing how you learn best can help them to help you!

1. How do I get information to stick in my head?
   a. seeing it

   b. listening to it

   c. touching it or manipulating objects (such as a puzzle)

2. What do I need from my teacher?
   a. lots of direction

   b. give me an assignment and let me figure out how to do it

   c. let me plan a whole project on my own

3. What grades would I get for nutrition, exercise and rest?
   a. an A or a B

   b. a C

   c. a D or an F

4. When do I do my best work?
   a. early morning

   b. after school

   c. evening

5. What's the best background noise when I'm studying?
   a. total quiet

   b. soft music

   c. rock music

6. What makes me work hardest?
   a. feel proud of myself

   b. gain approval from others

   c. achieve future goals

1. When possible, study using your best learning style. In class, pay closer attention when the information is presented in ways that are not your best for learning.

2. You'll need to adapt to different kinds of assignments. But when you have a choice, choose the type of assignment that suits you best.

3. You'll be a better student if you're eating healthy foods, exercising regularly and sleeping enough.

4. Schedule home study when you are rested and alert.

5. Do homework where you can control the background noise.

6. When the going gets rough, remind yourself of this answer to keep you going.

making the grade

Do you like school? Dislike it? Feel a little bit of both about it?

How much you like school is probably linked to how well you're doing. If you're making the grades your parents expect, you probably like it fine. If you're not doing well enough to please them, the pressure can turn you off school.

Maybe your parents expect an awful lot. They put so much pressure on you that you feel good grades are necessary to keep their love. Or maybe your parents are unaware how their "adult problems" at home are affecting your studies. They don't see their role in your falling grades, don't cut you any slack, don't get you any help.

Gentle pressure from your parents to do well in school can be helpful.

That kind of pressure is extreme, and it works against you. If you feel extreme pressure, talk about it with your parents, school counselor or other trusted adult.

However, if you feel gentle pressure to work hard in school, that can be helpful. It can give you the push you need to make your best effort even when the material is difficult or boring. Throughout your adult working life, you'll feel pressure to do well; school is a training ground for that. Learn now to cope with the stress that pressure causes and you'll be happier and healthier. (To review advice on handling stress, see page 33.)

If you are lucky enough to have some excellent teachers, learning will be easier and more fun. You may also have a teacher you think is unfair or not very good. If so, don't just give up and blame it on the teacher. That doesn't hurt the teacher; it only hurts you. You can not only survive a year with a bad teacher, you can manage to learn something. And next year you'll have different teachers.

Note: If you feel you're trying really hard in school, but you just don't understand the material, you may have a learning difference. Talk with your parents or a teacher about it. They can arrange to have you tested and, if necessary, helped by a trained counselor.

a story of harassment

Rick and his friends often razzed each other about their sexuality and boasted about the things they would do if they were ever alone with certain girls. Rick thought it was funny until the evening his sister Katie came home from school in tears. A group of boys in her class had made loud comments about her breasts as she passed them in the hallway. She was so upset that she was begging her parents to transfer her to a different school.

- If you were Katie, what would you like to say to the boys who made those comments?

- If you were Rick, what would you like to say to the boys who upset your sister?

- How should Rick and Katie's parents handle this situation?

- Should the school administration do anything? What would you suggest?

hallway harassment

Dirty jokes. Obscene gestures. Sexual remarks about your body. Unwelcome touching or grabbing as you walk down the hallway to class.

Those are all examples of sexual harassment. You may have seen it going on in your school. You may have experienced it yourself.

Some people think sexual harassment is a harmless "boys will be boys" thing and teens should just put up with it. They couldn't be more wrong. Sexual harassment causes a lot of pain and it is against the law. Victims — usually female, but sometimes male — may feel angry, helpless and scared.

Confronted about something they said or did that offended a girl, some boys will protest they were "only kidding," or "just fooling around."

How do you know if your words or actions are sexually harassing? Here's a simple test: Think about the females in your own family — your sister, cousin, mother. Is this the way you want other males to treat them?

Harassing a person makes him or her feel angry, helpless, scared.

Then remember that the girl you're harassing is someone else's sister or daughter.

Some boys also protest that certain girls "invite" sexual harassment by imitating the bimbo act they see in movies and on TV. They act openly sexy, wearing very tight or revealing clothing, coming on to boys in a big way.

These girls are mixed up about how they should behave, but that does not give boys the right to be disrespectful to them.

If you feel nervous or uncomfortable about the way other students are treating you at school, don't put up with it. Tell a teacher, counselor or administrator whom you trust. Everyone has the right to attend school in peace, and it is the school's job to make sure that this right is protected.

chapter 8

me + my world

the adult world

to tell or not to tell

getting involved

mentors + role models

the adult world

While you are growing up physically and emotionally during puberty, your mind is also maturing. You are better able to analyze information and figure things out using reason and logic. You are becoming more aware of people, issues and events beyond your childhood world of family, friends and school. You are entering the world of adults.

So it may surprise you to find that your new mental powers aren't making it any easier to understand the adult world; in fact, the world may seem more complex than ever! As a child you didn't ponder right and wrong or good and bad. There were simple answers, supplied by the important adults in your life. Now that you are older and wiser, you realize there are big arguments going on in the adult world, and sharp disagreements about what is right or wrong, good or bad, in politics, religion, morality and other matters.

Adults can disagree about right and wrong, good and bad.

You may hear adults arguing about controversial issues like gay marriage, abortion, and assisted suicide. They can sound angry, like they are fighting, and that can be scary. They can say things that make you wonder if what you believe is really true or right, and that can be confusing.

But if you listen and learn and think about what's going on in the adult world, you will be preparing yourself to participate in that world. You will be forming your own opinions, which may differ from the opinions of some family members, friends or classmates. You will be challenged to back up or defend your opinions when discussing them with others. Sometimes you will discover new facts or new ways of looking at an issue that will make you change your opinion.

In America, important controversial issues are argued and decided by the politicians that voters elect to make laws. When you are 18, you can vote for the candidates who best represent your opinions about right and wrong, good and bad. You will be alone in the voting booth, with no one to tell you what to do. You'll have to think for yourself. When you vote, you become an official member of the adult world.

if you witness a crime

If you witness a crime, here's what you should do:

1. Get to a safe place.

2. Tell what you saw to an adult you trust, a police officer, or the person who is in charge wherever you are at the time.

3. Write down all the details that you can

remember: exactly what you saw, who was involved, where you were, the time, what people were wearing, their hair color, height, weight, etc. If a car was involved, write down the license plate number.

4. Contact the police or the school principal.

If you are afraid to give your name, here are ways to report a crime anonymously — so no one will know it was you:

Call an anonymous tipline — Some police departments have 24-hour anonymous hot-lines. (In Philadelphia, it is 215-685-1137.)

If you can't find your local tipline, call the national WeTip hotline at 1-800-78-CRIME (1-800-782-7463). WeTip operators speak English and Spanish. They do not record your call and will not ask for your name. The oper-ator will pass on the information you give to your local police department. The operator will also give you a case number so that you can call back if you learn more information.

WeTip also accepts anonymous tips over the Internet. You can submit your tip at the Web site www.wetip.com.

Call 9-1-1 — When you call 9-1-1, the information you give will most likely be recorded and your phone number will be traced. So when the operator answers, clearly state that you would like to give your report *anonymously* and that you do *not* want a police officer to come to your home.

Call your local police district — If you believe that the crime is still in progress, or if you know that a crime regularly happens at a certain time and place, you can call into your local police district and make a "roll call complaint." You don't have to say who you are or what you saw. You can simply suggest that police should drive by a specific address or intersection. In this way, they can catch the criminals in the act. As with a 9-1-1 call, clearly state that you would like to remain anonymous.

Write a letter — Writing a detailed letter is a good way to anonymously tell the police or school principal what you know. Be sure to include all the information that you can remember. Some police departments and schools have drop boxes where you can leave your letter. Or, you can put your letter in the mail with no return address. You can look up the police address in a phone book or search for it on the Internet. Don't forget to put a stamp on your letter!

to tell or not to tell

We all want to feel that the neighborhoods where we live and go to school are safe. Rules and laws are important ways that cities, towns and schools keep people safe. Enforcing rules and laws is a tough job. To do it well, the few people who work as police officers and school principals need help from the many, many people who want the neighborhood to be safe.

But helping police officers and school principals to keep people safe is not always easy. Sometime, at school or in your neighborhood, you may witness someone breaking a rule or a law, and you will have to decide whether or not to tell. That can be a very tough decision.

People who break the law want you to think that telling makes you a "tattle-tale" or a "snitch." Those are just mean names they are using to try to keep you quiet so that they won't get caught and be punished.

Think about what will happen if you don't tell.

If you see people doing a bad thing, you know in your heart that helping the police or the principal to catch them and punish them would make your neighborhood feel safer —and that would be a good thing.

When deciding whether to tell, think about what might happen if you *don't* tell. For example, if you witness someone hiding a weapon, and you don't report it, the person could later use that weapon to hurt someone, maybe even someone you know. Or, if you see the wrong person getting blamed, he could be punished for something he didn't do.

If you think the bad thing you saw is really serious then you need to think really seriously about telling.

Even when telling is clearly the right thing to do, people who don't agree with your choice may criticize, tease, bully or ignore you. But there are bound to be more people who agree with your choice. Seek them out as friends. With their support, you can be a leader and explain to others why it is important for everyone to help keep your neighborhood safe.

If anyone threatens to hurt you if you tell, or because you told, you should report the threat right away to an adult you trust — a parent, teacher, guidance counselor or the police. It's their job to keep you safe.

133

how I could contribute

Here's a quiz that can help you figure out how to put your interests and skills to work as a volunteer. Put a check next to the activities that definitely interest you and a question mark next to the ones in which you might be interested.

___ Go door to door for a political candidate or cause.

___ Pick up trash for an environmental cleanup project.

___ Volunteer at a hospital or nursing home.

___ Work in a community garden project.

___ Raise money for a nonprofit organization.

___ Work behind-the-scenes stuffing envelopes or doing office work for an organization you support.

___ Deliver food to shut-ins or sick people.

___ Participate in a walkathon.

___ Hand out leaflets at a public place.

___ Counsel your peers about teen problems.

___ Tutor younger kids or help them with their homework.

___ Help collect clothes or toys or food items for a holiday collection drive.

Look at the things you marked. Did you choose:

☐ Projects built around big causes?
☐ Activities that focus on people as individuals?

☐ Tasks where you'd do physical work?
☐ Tasks that called for mostly brain power?

☐ Tasks where you'd persuade others to do something?
☐ Tasks where you'd lend a hand?

☐ Opportunities to meet strangers?
☐ Jobs for shy people?

getting involved

Chances are, your community faces problems, and your neighbors are trying to help. You could help, too. You could volunteer for a neighborhood cleanup. Or a political campaign. Or fund raising for a project that will make the world — our global community — a better place.

A wonderful thing about getting involved in your community is that you help yourself while helping others. You might make new friends. You might discover talents you never knew you had. You'll get a chance to express your values through action. You'll definitely get a break from the everyday routine of your home and school life.

You'll discover that by helping others you help yourself.

If you'd like to get involved, but don't know how, the first step is to think about your interests and talents.

Who or what are you interested in working with? There are so many choices: little children, the elderly, animals, the environment, the poor, the homeless, people with AIDS, and on and on.

Can you teach an illiterate person to read, entertain toddlers, cook, clean, repair things, tend a garden? Special talents are always welcome, but keep in mind that for most volunteer jobs the only requirement is a smile and your willingness to give of yourself.

Your answers to the questions above can help you figure out what kind of project you'd like to work on. Now, where to find such a project? Here are a few places to look:

• Your school guidance office.

• Your place of worship (church, temple, mosque, etc.).

• Your community newspaper; many list groups that need volunteers.

• The bulletin board at your local public library.

• The blue pages in your telephone book; human service agencies always need volunteers.

• On the Internet at www.liveunited.org or www.volunteermatch.org

learning from another's life

Think of some older person you like and respect. Now, try to list some questions you'd like to ask him or her. Here are a few to get you started.

• What were you like as a child? What things did you like to do?

• How did you figure out what you wanted to be when you grew up?
  When did you know?

• What were your favorite books when you were my age?

• If you could do anything over, what would it be?

• What did you like about school? What didn't you like?

• What kinds of problems have you had to deal with in your life?

• What do you think I do well? How do you think I could improve the things
  I don't do so well?

mentors + role models

Friends don't always have to be people your own age. An adult friend can be a valuable mentor to you.

The word mentor means wise and loyal counselor. A mentor gives a younger person the gift of his or her experience. The mentor's reward is your happiness and success.

Think of some adults besides your parents whom you admire: people who have earned your respect and trust. Maybe there's a teacher, a neighbor, a relative, or the parent of a friend. Already these people are role models for you. Because you admire them, you try to be like them.

But you might be wishing you could spend more time talking with them and getting their advice. If that's what you wish, you're wishing they could be mentors to you. Probably at least one of them can — and will, if you ask. Most adults would be delighted to spend time with a young person who looks up to them that way.

Note: A mentor should always have your best interests at heart. Anyone who tries to involve you in secret activities or a friendship that keeps you from your family and friends is up to no good. Some people may pretend to be mentors when they're really trying to use you for their own purposes. That's not mentoring you, that's exploiting, and you should stop spending time with that person.

An adult friend can give you the gift of greater experience.

How do you get someone to be your mentor? First, ask the person to please sit down with you some time to talk about school or friends or careers, or whatever you'd like to discuss. See how the person responds. If the first discussion is helpful, tell the person his or her advice meant a lot to you and you'd like to talk again sometime. If the person agrees, you've got yourself a mentor!

books & websites

For further reading:

Bell, Ruth. **Changing Bodies, Changing Lives** (Random House) 1998

Bourgeosis, Paulette and Wolfish, Martin, MD. **Changes in You & Me: A Book about Puberty Mostly for Boys** (Andrew and McNeal) 1998

Carey, Joely. **Body Changes** (Barron's Educational Series) 2006

Cobain, Bev. **When Nothing Matters Anymore: A Survival Guide for Depressed Teens** (Free Spirit Publishing) 2007

Cooper, Kenneth A. **Fit Kids! The Complete Shape up Program from Birth through High School** (Broadman & Holman Publishers) 1999

Harris, Robie H. **It's Perfectly Normal: Changing Bodies, Growing Up, Sex, and Sexual Health** (Candlewick Press) 2004

Jarosz, Jaqueline. **Dating with Confidence: A Teen's Survival Guide** (Adams Media Corporation) 2000

Madaras, Lynda and Madaras, Area. **The "What's Happening to My Body?" Book for Boys.** Also: **The "What's Happening to My Body?" Book for Girls** (Newmarket Press) 2007

Schaefer, Valorie Lee. **The Care & Keeping of You: The Body Book for Girls** (Pleasant Company) 1998

Swan-Jackson, Alys. **When Your Parents Split Up...How to Keep Yourself Together** (Price Stern Sloan) 1999

Woods, Samuel G. **Everything You need to Know about STDs** (Rosen Publishing) 2002

books & websites

You can use the Internet to get more information on some of the topics discussed in this book. Visit these addresses online.

www.familyplanning.org — information on family planning services in the Philadelphia area

www.sexetc.org — by teens, for teens, sponsored by the Network for Family Life Education at Rutgers University

www.cfoc.org — site of "Campaign for our Children," an abstinence-based teen pregnancy prevention program

www.kidshealth.org/kid — information on puberty, feelings and health issues for young teens, sponsored by the Nemours Foundation

www.goaskalice.columbia.edu — questions and answers about relationships, sex, substance abuse and health, sponsored by Columbia University

www.puberty101.com — pre-teens and teens ask questions about puberty and get honest, open answers

www.parent-teen.com — online magazine for families with teens

www.teenpregnancy.org — research, statistics and resources on teen pregnancy

www.advocatesforyouth.org — for teens and parents: information on sexuality, teen pregnancy prevention and other issues

www.girlshealth.gov — provides information about fitness, nutrition, relationships, drugs and alcohol, safety and emotions

www.youthlink.org — promotes youth empowerment, education and advocacy

www.ivyjoy.com — list of search engines that link to safe sites for kids

www.inhalants.org — comprehensive information on "huffing" compiled by the National Inhalation Prevention Coalition

www.childhelpusa.org — help for victims of child abuse from Childhelp USA, the organization behind the National Child Abuse Hotline

call for help

LOCAL NUMBERS — If you live in the Philadelphia area, you can get help by calling one of these local organizations.

Child Abuse Hotline in Pennsylvania: 24-hour toll-free hotline to report child abuse in Pennsylvania **800-932-0313**

CHOICE: Information about birth control, pregnancy tests, pregnancy, prenatal care, STDs, HIV, abortion, sexuality. English & Spanish **215-985-3300**

Philadelphia Domestic Abuse Hotline: 24-hour hotline and emergency shelter for women and children **866-SAFE-014**
(866-723-3014)

Suicide Prevention Center: 24-hour hotline that refers you to people in your area who can help you **215-686-4420**

The Attic Youth Center: Youth-run community center for gay, lesbian, bisexual, transgender and questioning youth **215-545-4331**

Women Organized Against Rape: 24-hour hotline in English and Spanish; also support groups and other programs for women, teens and victims of sexual abuse **215-985-3333**

Youth Emergency Service: 24-hour hotline; can provide temporary shelter for boys and girls 12-17 years old **215-787-0633**

call for help

NATIONAL NUMBERS — No matter where you live, you can get help by calling one of these toll-free numbers.

Alcohol and Drug Abuse: Hotline operated by the National Alcohol and Substance Abuse Information Center.............. **800-784-6776**

American Psychological Association (APA): Provides referrals to your state's APA for mental health concerns **800-964-2000**

CDC Hotline for STD/AIDS: Answers questions about STDs and gives referrals for doctors, clinics and further information. Refers HIV-positive people and STD-positive people to local services and supports groups all over the country.............. **800-CDC-INFO**
English & Spanish (800-232-4636)
TTY: 800-232-6348

Covenant House: Help for runaways and kids in crisis **800-999-9999**
TTY: 800-999-9915

National Child Abuse Hotline: Advice and referrals **800-4-A-CHILD**
(800-422-4453)

National Domestic Violence Hotline: Advice and referrals to help in your area when there is violence in your home....... **800-799-SAFE**
(800-799-7233)
TTY: 800-787-3224

Planned Parenthood: Advice and help with reproductive health, STDs and birth control **800-230-PLAN**
(800-230-7526)

RAINN Rape, Abuse and Incest National Network:
Provides counseling for victims **800-656-HOPE**
(800-656-4673)

DOODLES

just remember this

We've packed this book full of important information. You won't remember everything you've read, so keep the book handy and check back when you have a question or concern. For now, just remember these three things:

1. Talk to a trusted adult.

When you are worried or confused, talk to someone who cares about you, listens well, has earned your respect and will respect your privacy. A parent, older brother or sister, minister or clergy person, school counselor or health care provider might be a good choice.

2. Think before you act.

Things can happen quickly and unexpectedly. You may get an urge to do something daring or may feel pressured to act by someone else. In those situations, it's easy to make a mistake you will regret. Instead, pause for a second and ask yourself, "Does this feel right?" If the answer is no, stop.

3. Protect yourself.

The sexual choices you make now can have huge consequences, such as pregnancy or a serious disease. The only 100% sure way to avoid both is abstinence — not engaging in sexual behavior. If you decide to be sexually active, always use a condom to prevent disease and a birth control method to prevent pregnancy.

If you have sexual health questions or want to know how to get condoms and birth control methods, call the CHOICE hotline in Philadelphia: 215-985-3300 (English) or 215-985-3350 (Spanish) or 800-848-3367 (toll-free outside Philadelphia).